# Alcohol Addiction

A Self-help Guide to Get Free From Alcoholism

*(How to Extinguish Your Craving for Alcohol and Live a Healthy Life)*

**Angela Parker**

Published By **Regina Loviusher**

**Angela Parker**

All Rights Reserved

*Alcohol Addiction: A Self-help Guide to Get Free From Alcoholism (How to Extinguish Your Craving for Alcohol and Live a Healthy Life)*

**ISBN 978-1-77485-814-1**

No part of this guidebook shall be reproduced in any form without permission in writing from the publisher except in the case of brief quotations embodied in critical articles or reviews.

Legal & Disclaimer

The information contained in this ebook is not designed to replace or take the place of any form of medicine or professional medical advice. The information in this ebook has been provided for educational & entertainment purposes only.

The information contained in this book has been compiled from sources deemed reliable, and it is accurate to the best of the Author's knowledge; however, the Author cannot guarantee its accuracy and validity and cannot be held liable for any errors or omissions. Changes are periodically made to this book. You must consult your doctor or get professional medical advice before using any of the suggested remedies, techniques, or information in this book.

Upon using the information contained in this book, you agree to hold harmless the Author from and against any damages, costs, and expenses, including any legal fees potentially resulting from the application of any of the information provided by this guide. This disclaimer applies to any damages or injury caused by the use and application, whether directly or indirectly, of any advice or information presented, whether for breach of contract, tort, negligence, personal injury, criminal intent, or under any other cause of action.

You agree to accept all risks of using the information presented inside this book. You need to consult a professional medical practitioner in order to ensure you are both able and healthy enough to participate in this program.

**TABLE OF CONTENTS**

Introduction ......................................1

Chapter 1: Alcohol And Your Body ...7

Chapter 2: The Different Types Of Alcoholics ........................................22

Chapter 3: Following The Bar .........35

Chapter 4: What, When What, Which, Where And Who? What, Why, ................................................47

Chapter 5: Setting Boundaries........60

Chapter 6: Requires Regulating And Replacing .........................................75

Chapter 7: Getting Assistance.........96

Chapter 8: Recovery And A Path Moving Forward ............................111

Chapter 9: Times To Determine When To Stop Drinking Alcohol....127

Chapter 10: Clear Alcohol Essation Goals Alcohol Cessation................135

Chapter 11: Consult A Dentist ......148

Conclusion ...................................167

## Introduction

The alcohol is among the acceptable social substance available and is the most readily available to all people no matter what age. About three quarters of the population drink. For those who drink 70% of them work and their companies lose $181 billion in profits lost because of addiction-related issues. The causes of these problems range from injury to productivity loss, caused by frequent absences or inability to work.

Alcohol consumption is responsible for 29 percent of all fatalities in traffic during the year. In addition, alcohol is acknowledged as a cause for various kinds of cancer. Within the United States, alcohol accounts for a total of $252 billion dollars spent each year. These figures ought to be alarming and hopefully give you an opportunity to think about your drinking habits, dear reader.

If you're studying this text, it's most likely that you'd like to reduce the amount of alcohol you drink. Maybe there are family members or friends who are pushing the book onto your desk. The good news is that this book is about controlling and not quitting. A simple reduction in your consumption of alcohol by half could lead to improvement in your financial health, overall health, and your overall well-being. However, the first thing you should think about is where you're in the present. Are you looking to reduce your drinking habits for your health or your pocket? Are your relationship, job or your children in pain? Take note of how much you drink during a particular week.

A shocking details that most people ignore is the volume of a drink. A typical drink within the United States contains 0.6 ounces or 1.2 tablespoons of alcohol in pure form. 12 fluid ounces beer (5 percent alcohol content) eight ounces malt liquor (7 percent alcohol content) 5 glass ounces (flour) of wine (12 percent alcohol content) as well as an ounce and half of spirits with an 80 proof (40 percent alcohol percentage) are all considered to be one drink. That means that a six-pack of cans of 18 ounces of beer is actually nine typical drinks. Most people don't are aware of how much math is involved until they calculate it for themselves. This can cause anxiety or shock for those who do not be aware of how much alcohol they actually consumed.

A healthy amount of alcohol for those who must drink, is one standard-sized drink each day for women and two drinks per day for males, based on the same measurements as above. With the many different alcohol percentages in various drinks, and the various types of drinks on the market that's why how many people drink more than they intend to. Mixed drinks usually have more alcohol in them than many believe since every shot of spirit equals one drink of standard. Drinks that have a variety of alcohol can be as much as at least three to four beverages by itself.

A very crucial factors to be aware of is the amount you spend on alcohol. There are many people who decide to quit once they realize how much their drinking habits are costing them. An estimate of a cheap alcohol or wine could be around $5 for a standard unit, a six pack, one bottle and so on. If you purchase one bottle each night, it's about $35 per week, and $1,820 for the year. While this might be a shock wake-up call for somepeople, it's important to confront yourself about the habit or the habits that have grown around drinking. If you do not know these in lots details, the odds of reducing your drinking will are slim. If you're honest with your family, yourself and your acquaintances You can establish the necessary support to manage your alcohol intake instead of letting it dominate your life.

Consumption: What is To Much?

The issue of whether or not you should drink is a controversial one at times. There are certain people who should never drink alcohol: people who are under the age limit set by legal system (21 within the U.S.) and women who are pregnant or attempting to get pregnant; people using prescription drugs, or purchased over the counter and that might not mix well with alcohol; those working on tasks that require concentration, focus as well as alertness (i.e. driving) or recovering alcoholics among some. If you struggle to say that no, or controlling the amount of the amount of alcohol you're drinking it is best to abstain from drinking whenever you are able. There are more harmful drinking habits like excessive drinking or binge drinking that shouldn't be routinely practiced.

Binge drinking typically involves ingestion of lots of alcohol over a brief amount of time. It is often seen at parties, bars or other social events where alcohol-based drinks are served. This kind of behavior is often seen in young drinkers, specifically students in college or who are just reaching legally drinking age. Binge drinking can be defined as drinking four or more beverages at one time for women, and five or more for males. Keep in mind that a typical drink isn't defined by the amount of glasses one sips however, it is measured by the quantity of alcohol in every drink.

The term "heavy drinking," which is most commonly experienced by alcoholics it is defined as having at least eight drinks every week for women, as well as 15 to more drinking per week for males. The reason drinking heavily a problem is the way it sneaks in on someone. It is not a goal to drink more than a dozen drinks every week. It's a gradual process as tolerance grows and it often occurs without aware of. A night you're high after only two glasses of beer or wine. After a week you could need three. Two weeks later then you'll need four. Perhaps in the coming month, you'll require an alcoholic drink before you go to going to bed.

Alcoholism is a gradual progression with a steady increase very few people plan in advance but it could spiral out of control in the blink of an eye. One method to stop this issue from growing exponentially is to set limitations on the amount you are allowed to drink on a particular day. There are also rules regarding when and what you are allowed to drink, or perhaps the manner in which you can spend your money on drinks. A couple of simple guidelines and a little control can allow an drinker get a step away from the cliff. It's a great beginning step to reduce.

## Chapter 1: Alcohol And Your Body

"Alcohol is an allergy to the body as well as an obsession in the mind. ."--Rita Mae Brown

Alcohol has a myriad of effects on our body. Drinking alcohol impacts every body part in some way or another. Since it is the second most utilized substance, next to tobacco, it's not surprising that we're aware of the harm it can cause. While the long-term effects are generally given plenty of attention, alcohol consumption also has short-term impacts. One of the most noticeable short-term effects could be the hangover.

Hangovers trigger issues like the sensitivity towards light diarrhea, vomiting, extreme dehydration, in addition to other issues. Drinking alcohol can cause drastic shifts in body's glucose levels, which can lead to problems like hypoglycemia. This is caused by blood sugar levels falling rapidly because alcohol that is rich in sugar is transformed. In addition, nausea, dizziness and headaches due to the low blood sugar level can make the effects of a hangover more severe.

Drinking causes disruption to many neural pathways that run through the brain, particularly those involved with communication. This means that various areas of the brain are unable to communicate as effectively once someone has begun drinking. The lack of communication within the brain results in slow reaction times, less coordination and difficulty communicating with others. Poor decision-making occurs when the brain isn't able to effectively communicate as it is required.

Alcohol consumption can also have an a negative effect on sleep. While many believe that drinking alcohol can help get sleep but this isn't the case. Actually, drinking can cause low quality of sleep. Instead of allowing the rapid movement of your eyes (REM) sleep which helps our bodies rest by reducing your nervous system. In the end, even although someone might be able to fall asleep quicker but they don't remain in bed.

As opposed to REM sleeping, which is supposed to occur later in the cycle of sleep the body is more likely to remain asleep in non-REM mode. Sleeping in non-REM causes people to wake more frequently and is more difficult to get back to sleep. To fall asleep when drunk is also a challenge. While drinking alcohol can make you exhausted, it does so in a way that is not natural which can result in a decrease in level of rest. In addition to the simple getting up after a sleepless night, a night following a drink isn't exactly relaxing or beneficial for the body. This could lead to excessive fatigue and sluggishness.

Drinking can raise the body's temperature by raising your heartbeat and also expanding blood vessels. Although this can make people who drink feel more comfortable and more comfortable, the heat is absorbed rapidly across the body. This causes the body's temperature to drop much more quickly after it has risen. The body is also severely dehydrated after drinking alcohol.

The short-term effects of alcohol are not always immediate and negative. These are just some of the main reasons why people are more attracted to alcohol. An euphoric feeling and a decrease in anxiety could enhance the perception that some people have of their own or others who are around them. This is the reason many people are fun drinking and appear as if they are. The drawback to all these negative effects the reality is that they will not last long. The fact that someone is less stressed after drinking doesn't mean that they are free of anxiety. The temporary feeling of euphoria is not enough to make you the talk of the night.

The decrease in inhibitions can be among the most harmful in the short term. If someone drinks they're less likely make good choices. They may think that poor choices are better ones. This leads to situations like one-night-stands or car accidents, as well as other injuries caused by alcohol. When someone is dancing on the table or getting in a car after having a couple of drinks, their lower inhibitions are in play.

If someone drinks often, there is an immense disconnect between their mind and body. This can lead to poor choices, such as drinking another drink, placing bets with someone else or engaging in the middle of a fight in a bar. The brain gets swollen because of the alcohol absorption through the bloodstream. The slower speed of communication, the slurred voice blurred vision and other effects of alcohol can be very heavy on the mind of an alcohol user. The problem is these regrets can only be felt later.

At the time the drinker can see almost all the harm they may cause. They aren't aware that they appear or sound stupid. Someone who is drunk may not be able to read the body language in the right way. This issue can cause many issues, particularly in public places like the bar. One who is drunk may believe that the person next to them is flirting rather than being extremely uncomfortable. They might not realize the bartender's suggestion that they reduce their speed. They might not even realize that the person at the table of pool is pushing them to slow down.

These memories and signals might take a long time to reach the brain of an alcoholic, if they ever happen to occur. Most likely, the person who is drunk is likely to leave the bar after a long night of drinking without a single recollection. What they'll be left with to remember their evening is headaches and a empty wallet in the best case scenario. The worst-case scenario could result in destruction to the vehicle or body. In the end, it's even more dangerous to lose little bits of memory, rather than completely blackout.

Imagine this: You've woken after an evening of drinking, and you're unsure of your thoughts. You were stumbling to the bathroom, and had difficulty keeping your balance, however, you were able to get there. Then, you were grabbed by someone. Your brain fails to complete the thought. Then you are left wondering whether you were the victim of an attack or even if you could have hurt someone else, but you really could have done something else. Perhaps someone was helping you to get to a taxi, or get to home. Even if everything was innocent, you'll never be able to tell for certain since the brain is able to only supply small fragments of information. The brain isn't the only organ which is affected alcohol.

Alcohol and Organs

Alcohol circulates throughout the bloodstream, reaching large number of organs within the body.

It begins to disintegrate when it is placed in the mouth, and then it goes down your throat , and eventually into the digestive system. A small portion of every drink is absorbed into the stomach as well as the small intestine, with the majority of alcohol being absorbed into the small intestine, if there is no food within the stomach. If someone drinks following eaten the stomach's pyloric valve remains closed in order in order to let the food be digested. This restricts the access of alcohol into the small intestinal. All the alcohol that is taken in is then absorbed into the bloodstream. This allows accessibility to all parts your body, which includes important organs, like the brain. A majority of what you drink however, is processed in the liver.

It is also the biggest organ of the human body. It is located right under your ribs, on the upper left side of your abdomen. It is responsible for the processing of nutrients and medicines and energy, as well as eliminating toxins, aiding in the formation of blood clots and also making bile that aids in the process of fats, as well as absorbing alcohol. While there are many aspects that could alter this figure it is believed that the liver breaks down an average of one drink per hour. Any additional alcohol consumed during the time frame is absorbed into the blood stream, causing the feeling of being intoxicated.

The majority of the alcohol found inside the liver gets converted into an enzyme known as alcohol dehydrogenase (ADH) that transforms the alcohol into the acetaldehyde. Another enzyme, the aldehyde deshydrogenase (ALDH) is responsible for metabolizing the Acetaldehyde to Acetate. Acetate is then further processed to finally leave the body in carbon dioxide and as water. If the blood alcohol level is extremely high There is an alternate process that activates an entirely different group of enzymes. This is called the microsomal ethanol-oxidizing system. The system basically does the same type of breakdown, but it is equipped to handle greater quantities.

Yet, no person regardless of size or gender can adequately process each drink that could enter it. The negative effects of drinking can become more grave. Drinking excessively can lead to stomach ulcers known as peptic. It may reduce the pancreas' capacity to make insulin, which could lead to diabetes or cause the pancreas to get inflammation-prone, leading to pancreatitis. The diuretic effect of alcohol is raising the quantity of urine. It can alter the kidneys filtering and regulation processes, resulting in dehydration.

Alcohol can be absorbed by the brain within 30 seconds after drinking. It targets brain's nerve cells as well as the cerebral cortex. It alters the way the brain thinks and interprets things. That's why those who have consumed just a little bit may believe it's an appropriate idea to hug a stranger, or to get behind the steering wheel of a car. Alcohol can have a significant impact on memory too which can cause the occurrence of blackouts, increased aggression and hallucinations as well as fatigue.

Consuming too much in one go or drinking a lot over a long time could cause an irregular heartbeat also known as arrhythmia. The change in a person's normal heartbeat could result in elevated blood pressure and also excessive stretching and/or drooping the heart muscle, a condition known as cardiomyopathy. All of these issues and harm to the heart can lead to stroke, which can be fatal.

The liver is responsible for the metabolism of alcohol consumed, it is the organ that is the most affected. Consuming too much alcohol can harm liver cells forever, turning the normal tissues into scar tissue. This affects the liver's ability to properly absorb nutrients and can result in an increase in the accumulation of fat. This type of damage can also affect the liver's capacity to eliminate contaminants in the human body. It can lead to liver failure, jaundice or even cancer.

In the words of the National Cancer Institute: "There is a consensus in the scientific community that alcohol consumption can cause different kinds of cancer. The Report on Carcinogens, the National Toxicology Program of the US Department of Health and Human Services mentions consumption of alcohol as a human carcinogen that is well-known.

The evidence suggests that the greater amount one consumes--and especially the more alcohol one drinks frequently over time, the greater chances of developing an alcohol-related cancer.

Even those who drink no greater than one bottle a day and who are binge drinkers (those who drink more than four drinks for women, and 5 or more beverages in men in a single sitting) are slightly more at risk of developing a risk of certain cancers. Based on the data from 2009 the study estimated that 3.5 percent of all cancer deaths across the United States (about 19,500 deaths) were caused by alcohol.

Alcohol is known to cause a range of cancers. Liver cancer is the most prominent concern since it is the organ most accountable for handling alcohol within the body. Alcohol consumption can result in throat, mouth, esophageal, as well as laryngeal cancer. All of these, too are real concerns because drinking can affect the mouth, throat as well as all of its components first. Risks of developing colon and rectal cancer is increased among people who drink heavily. It has also been associated with pancreatic cancer, prostate cancer and melanoma.

Alcohol can also have an adverse effect on the calcium balance within the body and making vitamin D. Both are vital for bone health. Calcium helps keep bones healthy as well as vitamin D, among the elements that helps your body to absorb calcium. Alcoholism can also raise cortisol levels. Cortisol is believed to accelerate the destruction of bones and reduce the development of bone. Because of these hormone changes injuries, falls, and fractures are more frequent in those who drink heavily, with a particular focus on the spine or hip fractures.

Alcohol and Calories

The calories contained in alcohol usually are not noticed by people who consume them. In reality, the alcohol's calories are thought as empty, which means they are not nutritionally valuable. There aren't any vitamins, minerals or other nutrients are required to function properly are present, just sugar and alcohol. This is made evident when looking at the nutritional information on an alcohol-based drink. The only thing listed are sugar, calories and carbs. These extra calories need to be used somewhere and this is the reason for drinking alcohol with weight increase. However, how much alcohol are you actually drinking?

Wine is generally seen as a relatively low-calorie drink. The actual calories, however, can vary between 100-100 calories for champagne, to around 160 calories for sweetness or dessert wine. It amounts to a serving. It means that a person who consumes three glass of wine, has consumed the equivalent of half of a chocolate cake. A whole bottle of wine can be equivalent to the calories as a hamburger with multiple patties.

A pint of lager contains between 100-150 calories, with heavier beers such as stout, containing additional calories. A single pint is the same as a medium-sized slice of pizza. Also, someone who consumes a six-pack of 16-ounce drinks has consumed about the same amount of calories as the entire pizza.

Mixed drinks can have more calories as a result of sugary mixers, or cola , in combination with the alcohol. A frozen margarita is calorie equivalent to a cheeseburger (300 calories in the average.) Like all of the drinks we've discussed the calorie count increases with the more alcohol consumed. Four drinks that are standard in one go can result in the same amount of calories that two big hot dogs.

These numbers also make it difficult for the majority of people to follow or investigate. Calorie amounts are not always readily accessible. They're printed on multi-packs of boxes, however, not within individual bottles. In bars, this information is not always available unless the customer is asked and the bartender knows where to find it. Calculations of calories and other data could not be able to account for the modifications that could be applied to any drink or food order. Even if a single drink contains just 70 calories, it does not necessarily mean that the amount will be the same when drinks, shots, or a different kind or amount of alcohol has been added into the drink. In general, staying healthy when drinking alcohol is a struggle at best.

If you're looking to remain healthy over the long-term the best choice is to limit or stop drinking. There are numerous studies that have created a great list of what alcohol causes on the human body. Each major organ is affected in a way or another by the alcohol's absorption into blood.

The liver and brain are both very damaged after excessive drinking, and some of the damage will never be healed. Whatever the reasons you may have for wanting to limit your alcohol intake think about your body first before asking yourself what exactly you're doing to it.

## Chapter 2: The Different Types Of Alcoholics

"Ignorance is similar to alcohol. The more you drink and the more you're not capable of recognizing its effects on your ."--Jay Bylsma

The first step once you know what alcohol can do to your body, is to take a an open look at your daily life. Examine your spending habits on alcohol, your drinking habits as well as the people that surround you. This is an important one. crucial. Have anyone who are around you expressed concern over the alcohol you drink? Do they favor drinking? There are those who believe that people be influenced by the behavior and morals from the people who they are spending the longest time with. This could be something worth taking into consideration for those trying to limit their alcohol consumption.

There are a variety of factors that affect the amount an alcohol user spends on their drink, which includes the kind of alcohol they consume as well as the location they drink from, and how much they drink. The price of wine is usually higher per serving in time than beer. The cost of being constantly drunk is higher over the course of just one or two instances of excessive drinking when a person's tolerance increases. Bars cost much more than drinking inside your house. Mix drinks are more alcoholic and dependent on what you drink it might be less booze-like making it more difficult to know how much alcohol one consumes.

Another factor to take into consideration is the kind of person you could be. Experts in the area of addiction have identified five kinds that include young adults, interfamilial, antisocial functional, chronic, and severe. The five categories are classified by age, how often they drink, the likelihood they will seek treatment for their alcoholism and what treatment might be the best fit for them, in addition to other aspects. The identification of your type can aid you in managing your alcohol dependence.

The most common type of alcoholic is young adult. This is the most popular type of alcohol in the United States, with 32 percent of those who drink falling into this category of young adult. People in the young adult group tend to begin drinking between 19 and 20 years old, and their average age is about 25. The men in this category tend to be single and outnumber women by 2.5 or 1.0. They don't typically have other issues with substance abuse or any history of drinking within the family. They drink the equivalent of the equivalent of 143 days per year. They prefer 12-step programs over private rehabilitation, perhaps because of the social aspect.

An antisocial young person is not yet in their mid-twenties, however, they are more likely to begin drinking earlier, usually around the mid teens. Nearly half of young drinkers who are antisocial have had a drinking history within the family. The onset of their own alcohol-related habits is within the first 2 years after they begin drinking. The people in this group are also more likely to have mental health issues. The symptoms may be a range of conditions, from antisocial personality disorder to obsessive compulsive disorder , to major depression.

Substance abuse is a common occurrence among young alcoholics who are antisocial; the majority of them are addicted to amphetamines and opioids as well as marijuana, or cocaine. A majority users smoke. They typically consume five or more beverages in one go and consume an average of 200 days over the course of a year. They have the least optimistic outlook for recovery. Treatments for them must be most severe and more likely to require a complete withdrawal from drugs, instead of cutting back or implementing other methods of control.

Functional alcoholics are typically wealthy and well-educated, with excellent homes. They tend to be in denial about their alcohol-related issues and are more likely to excuse themselves. They typically begin drinking at a young age, usually about 18 however, they don't start to drink until they are in when they reach their 30s. While smoking is common among Functional alcoholics however they generally do not suffer from other addictions. One quarter of functional addicts have been diagnosed as having depression.

The main issue with functional alcoholism is that they are reluctant to admit their addiction. Because they don't display obvious signs of a severe alcoholism those in this category are difficult to recognize when you don't live with them. If they seek assistance, which only 17% of them do those who are alcoholics, they will go to the 12-step program and private counseling. The focus of their recovery is on getting back to healthier levels, or even complete abstinence.

Intermediate family alcoholics begin drinking around the age of 17, are middle-aged and begin to develop alcohol-related behaviors by the time they reach their 30s. A majority of them have an alcoholism family history. The majority of them have smoked, with the majority of them consuming marijuana and cocaine. More than one-quarter of family alcohol addicts have sought treatment to overcome their addiction. They seek help from their health providers as well as self-help groups or detox groups, as well as other programs for treatment.

The last group is the chronically severe alcohol users. The majority of them are middle-aged and began drinking at the age of 16 years old. The majority smoke and are diagnosed with co-occurring disorders like depression and anxiety and bipolar disorders. Alcoholics of this type consume alcohol for 248 days during a particular year. One quarter of those in this group will eventually get divorced. A mere 10% of people went to college, and only half of them are employed full-time. Any treatment that is prescribed for chronically severe alcoholics should address their other issues and incorporate treatments to prevent relapses.

Drinking Habits

Your drinking habits include the time, place you drink, and the way you do it in addition to other factors. When you look at these habits, you can identify the behaviors that need to be changed to to limit the amount of alcohol you consume. If you drink with friends, you may have to alter the location they go to work and avoid a trip to the bar at the end of their shift, and instead going to a cafe instead. If you drink at home in the evening or before sunset, could take a break from home without cash in the bank to purchase alcohol to reduce their consumption. They could also use the time with their family members to remind them why they're trying to reduce their drinking. It is essential to be aware of the triggers that cause you to drink and to keep them you control.

If you drink regularly when you are stressed, it might be worthwhile to look into other ways to manage your mood. The practice of mindfulness or meditation could be helpful and remind yourself that you are able to manage yourself and your responses to situations. If others are making you feel angry, you may decide to let the anger out rather than burying it away in bottles. No matter what your habits are all people with problems with drinking has these habits. It is likely that you drink the same kind of alcohol because of the same reasons each time. If you look at the causes and triggers, you will be able to effectively cut down. Be sure to engage in more appropriate behaviour while trying to reduce your intake.

A weekend night out after all your daily obligations are considered to be more acceptable than having a drink during lunch breaks from work, or any similar activity. Such irresponsibility can cause you to be fired or hurt or even hurt another person. It's acceptable, however driving to drink more alcohol after having had a drink isn't. If you're engaged in these risky activities or if drinking causes you to lose your anger, you should think about cutting down in order to protect your personal security and the safety of those who are around you. There are many triggers that are within your control.

Track how much alcohol you are able to consume. You might want to set a daily limit on yourself, especially in the case of drinking at home. You should then be sure to be sure to stick to your amount. If you need to, give your debit or cash card over to the person you live with, and do not reclaim them until the next shift. Every habit or action that you are prone to, there's a solution If you're looking closely enough. Whatever you drink now If you really want to curb your drinking the book could aid you in doing this.

The Stages of Alcohol Dependence

The term "alcohol use disorder" is the term applied to a person's drinking habits that creates a lot of distress or damage in their life. It is typical when a person must drink more alcohol than usual in order to feel the similar consequences. It is possible that they are unable to function without drinking and it can affect their the daily routine. People who drink may be perceived as selfish because of their inability to stop drinking the alcohol. However, this is not the case.

Two indicators that suggest that alcohol dependence is the need to drink more to achieve the similar result. The other indication is that you are experiencing withdrawal symptoms when alcohol is eliminated. These symptoms can include anxiety or tremors, nausea, confusion as well as a racing heart and sleepiness. The withdrawal symptoms can hinder a person's ability perform. Each of these stages could trigger withdrawal symptoms. The degree of withdrawal will depend on the severity of alcoholism.

The lowest amount of alcohol-related abuse is known as early alcohol dependence. It can be difficult to discern or anticipate what it could turn into. The people at this stage will typically learn about various types of alcohol, and tend to be experimenters. They are likely to try a broad assortment of drinks. They are also social drinkers who will consume a lot of drinks as a means to party.

A few people are never able to get past this point in their alcohol consumption, and drink only when they are in social situations or at celebrations. However, this does not shield them from the many health consequences of drinking alcohol. However, those who get past this stage and begin drinking more frequently and in greater quantities are more likely to have an alcohol-related history within the family. Other genetic or environmental factors may play a role.

The next stage of alcohol abuse is determined by the amount of alcohol consumed and also by the intention behind the ingestion. That is, those who suffer from alcohol addiction issues will consume alcohol with the ultimate goal being drunkenness. People with these issues have physical mental, emotional, or emotional cravings for alcohol. These people are most likely withdrawal symptoms if disconnected of their supply. Anyone who plans to stop cold turkey need to be supervised by a medical professional.

The link between drinking alcohol and the drinker can't be overlooked at this point. The need for alcohol becomes so in the body that withdrawal symptoms are very likely. Additionally, there is a greater number of excuses for drinking and an increase in dependence on alcohol. People who are dependent on alcohol are less likely to stay away from regular consumption and tend to never get off a glass half-full. These people are also more likely show symptoms of severe alcohol dependence and signs of the same.

The third stage is serious alcoholism. These are the people who function well and are the most likely to be. They cover up the majority of their drinking , or perform effectively enough to make others not even suspect. However, they aren't immune to the harm they do for their bodies. They may still be suffering from anemia or gout or any other illness that are aggravated or caused by alcohol.

The end-stage stage of alcohol abuse is the most devastating stage, and the people who are in it have lost all of their faith. They tend to be extremely self-damaging and more likely to be to drink to live than drinking to live. At this point it's less painful to drink more rather than doing anything other than that. The withdrawal process can cause severe discomfort and organs are often failing in the patients. People who suffer from this condition are at an increased risk of self-harming and, often, are trying to experience something other that the constant feeling of numbness that is caused by alcohol.

Even with alcohol abuse that is at the end of its course there's an opportunity to get better. Although it may be difficult but the outcomes are worth it. The decision to stop drinking, or cutting down, can have incredible effects on one's overall health. In some instances cutting back too early could help organs recover from injury.

Whatever kind of addict you are, or the type of treatment you select there is always a chance to recover from addiction if you are willing to take the process seriously. It's not going to be always easy however, it's not impossible. If you begin with a plan to decrease your alcohol intake, rather than completely quit you could be more than successful. Understanding the kind of alcoholic you are as well as the stage you may be at can assist. The outlined options can guide you to the kind of treatment and support that will help you.

**Chapter 3: Following The Bar**

"Millions of deaths wouldn't be happening if not because of the drinking of alcohol. Similar can be said about the millions of births ."--Mokokoma Mokhonoana

Drinking alcohol has a greater cost in comparison to the pocket. The cost could be through the loss of life, be it due to drinking-related accidents in the car, poisoning by alcohol or a dysfunctional family life due to drinking. These risks are often the ones that cause people to be cautious when it comes to excessive drinking. Drinking alcohol can be the least risky of possible outcomes because, at the very least, is an alcohol user performing something for themselves , not involving other people.

The majority of alcohol poisoning cases are resulted from binge drinking, or having more than eight to ten average drinks in one drinking session. Alcohol consumption results in 95,000 deaths across the U.S. each year, which is equivalent to 261 people dying every single day.

Most of the deaths are Caucasian males who have an average age of around 35. Deaths that occur in this manner are thought to live for the average of 29 years as per the Centers for Disease Control (CDC).

The signs of alcohol poisoning are the slowness of breathing, which is lower than 8 breaths per minute. There is also the gap of at least 10 seconds between breaths. The people who suffer from alcohol poisoning might experience extreme nausea, confusion, and vomiting. They might experience seizures, fall asleep or struggle to awake. Due to the effects of alcohol on our body's temperature a person who is suffering from alcohol poisoning might develop clammy skin, and even hypothermia. In extreme cases an alcoholic might be unable to breathe, fall into a coma and eventually end up dying.

When an individual is overdosing on alcohol the body is flooded with liquid alcohol that your brain starts to shut down the basic functions. This includes respiration, heart rate and the control of temperature. If someone is stricken due to drinking, they might be unable to breathe because of their saliva or vomit, and then die from asphyxiation. All of this could be made more difficult by the use of medications or substances which do not work with alcohol. Even if someone does not die due to alcohol poisoning, they can be afflicted with brain injury.

Alcohol poisoning and its related dangers can be prevented by reducing the amount of alcohol consumed or eating food to help the body process it, as well as avoiding mixing the use of illegal drugs and alcohol in addition to other. Although, as mentioned above, the effects of alcohol poisoning are an untimely death and is a tragedy, this is at the very least the alcohol user being a victim. When someone is drunk and makes poor choices it is possible that they take driving a vehicle or return to a shattered home and cause more harm and heartache. The consequences of drinking excessively can affect everyone in the alcohol-related person's life, with certain people more than others. It could even endanger lives that are not the alcohol-related one. Drinking heavily can cause the death in innocent victim.

Drunk Driving

Alcoholics can alter the life of someone who has never met as a result of a crash caused by drunk driving. Twenty-eight people die in drunk driving accidents every day. Since alcohol can affect the brain, reflexes, as well as vision, it can seriously affect a driver's ability to safely drive. Even before reaching the levels that are recognized as drunk, someone who's had a drink can be unable to complete two tasks simultaneously. The diminished attention span and inability to keep track of moving objects will only become worse as they drink more eventually rendering even the thought of driving nearly impossible.

A third of traffic deaths are caused by drunk drivers. Furthermore, as high as one quarter of motorists feel secure driving after having as little as three drinks. If you've had three drinks and are but not legally drunk for bigger drivers, drivers have significantly less control of their eye coordination. They may suffer from memory loss of a short duration and could be unable to operate their vehicle properly particularly in an emergency. This is the reason for 209,000 injuries each year as a result of impaired driving.

Drinking and driving while impaired can result in damage to property and incur legal fees in addition. If you are charged for driving while intoxicated (DUI) as well as driving drunk (DWI) have a four-fold higher chance receive a second conviction or even lose their life. If someone is charged with several charges, they might be required to have an alcohol breathalyzer fitted to their vehicle. This device is to ensure safety in the event of an emergency and requires that the driver blow a small BAC amount (usually .02 at most) for the purpose of starting the vehicle.

These breathalyzers, often referred to by the name ignition interlock device can stop the car from beginning when alcohol is detected on the breath of the driver. They usually comprise a handheld unit and a mouthpiece with a removable design, and an extension cord for relays that connects to an ignition. They require a precise pattern of breath pressure, strength and volume. It is typical to have a specific pattern be needed, like sucking in, blowing it out, sucking and then sucking out again. The patterns can differ between devices. next.

These tests are also conducted periodically while the vehicle is operating. It is recommended that drivers stop whenever it is safe in order to perform the additional breathalyzer tests. If a test ever unsuccessful, the car cannot begin if it's not operating. If it's running, the vehicle could flash lights, honk its horn, notify police, or perform any of these. Additionally, to all of this, the setting up of the breathalyzer is typically carried out at no expense to the car owner.

Another aspect to take into consideration when assessing drunken driving concerns the fact that there are people in the vehicle. A majority of the people polled by the CDC said that they were in the car with a drunk driver often because they were drunk. In the majority of cases they had a connection with the drunk driver and believed that they were safe to drive. This is a common misconception--everyone thinks they are a safer driver than they are, even before alcohol is brought up for consideration. This behavior can increase the body count in the case of an accident.

However safe a driver you believe you are, remember to be aware of your choices regarding alcohol and driving. If you've been drinking and driving, you're statistically more secure taking a taxi or having a designated driver get home instead of driving. This is true even after just one drink. Being involved in an accident can cause damages to your property, legal costs and even a whole life.

Alcohol and the Home

Research has shown that the use of alcohol and violence in the intimate relationship often occur in conjunction. It could be any behavior that harms the spouse, which could include physical or emotional abuse, sexual assault as well as verbal abuse. Alcohol is an excuse often in these scenarios: "I was drunk and angry." While not all who is a user of alcohol or drugs goes into a relationship of abuse but there is an association that can't be ignored. A majority of those who abuse drugs don't commit violence due to their addiction to drugs, however their habits can contribute to domestic violence.

Substance abuse is a factor in the 40%- 60% range instances of domestic violence according to numerous studies. This suggests the close relationship between the two issues. Substance abuse in women who live in an abusive relationship is two times as likely as women who do not reside living in a hostile home. It could be the victim's personal decision, maybe to ease the pain of her partner, or could be a result of coercion from her abuser. This is a typical strategy to ensure that the victims feel just as happy as they feel, right now in the same way that the perpetrator thinks they do.

Of course, it isn't just a problem for women, and it isn't committed solely by males. Spousal abuse, as with alcohol abuse, is committed by any sex. The addition of alcohol can make a situation more difficult. If the victim also looks for alcohol to soothe the pain or escape from the issue the result is two alcohol-related people in the home and no one has control or the ability to think clearly. It turns into a powder keg.

Numerous studies have revealed that those who participate in domestic violence will take part in the abuse after having drinking one or more times which suggests that the amount of drunkenness isn't an element. It is also possible to have a relationship with their partner but without alcohol in their system. The effects of alcohol can affect the abuser's perception of a circumstance, as well as their response towards their partner. It is possible that they feel more powerful or more in control following a drink or two, leading to the desire for their partner to follow. If drinking has become an issue in their relationship, possibly because of finances at home drinking could increase the tension.

Drinking heavily can cause a serious decline in self-control, which may lead to increased aggression or decreased inhibitions. It can lead to sexual abuse in addition to physical abuse, and is often reported by students in college. Alcohol can dull shyness and negate any notion of conformity to guidelines, leading to an increase in confidence and loosening of inhibitions. The confidence that is heightened may be way too high because of drinking, resulting in expectations of total respect from the partner. If someone believes this, however has no one to share it with could be in a more dire situation and expecting the same from someone who owes nothing. This is another instance in which domestic violence or sexual violence is a frequent consequence.

The abuses are often not reported or are not reported due to a lack of recall of the events or a fear that other people will not believe the story. It is not even considering different possibilities, like the perpetrator threatening their victim to not speak. Another reason why people don't report their abuse is disbelief about what actually happened. It is usually experienced in the first time of occurrences or victims who are younger. They might not realize they've been victimized, or they may not be able to report because they fear that people will regard them with disdain or resentment.

The effects of alcohol on the mind and body have caused it to be misused by people who suffered harm previously, maybe someone who was sexually or physically victimized in the early years of their life. Alcohol used to cover up the effects of stress or pain can only be effective for a short time and is cannot be sustained in the long run. In the end, when tolerance to alcohol increases, an individual is likely to need to drink more to achieve the same result. This is the reason that those who have suffered abuse are prone to using alcohol in order to forget their troubles. This vicious cycle leads to more drinking.

Anyone who might be engaging in domestic violence due to drinking ought to seek help from a professional immediately. This is among the most severe consequences that can be triggered by a alcohol-related lifestyle. As with many other extreme situations, this could eventually cause death for the victim if the person who is a victim of abuse does not seek help at the appropriate time. Anger and alcohol are an unwise combination, and no one should be taking it to their spouse. Alcohol consumption to solve marital issues isn't a solution; it's more like closing a wound from a gun by using a band-aid.

With all the potential negative effects, damage and the other people who could be hurt due to a single drinking routine, it's extremely vital to analyze the habits with complete transparency. What is the amount of alcohol you consume frequently? How much do you pay for this addiction? How will you behave when you've been drinking? How do you treat your partner or family members? Do you have any friends who are honest with you about the post-drinking behavior?

There are a variety of strategies that can be employed to help people cut down on their drinking , and minimize the effects that follow from this harmful habit. Abstaining from drinking and drinking less are two completely different strategies however they may produce the same results in the short-term of improving your lifestyle. Maybe cutting back may lead to total abstinence in the future. If the harm you're doing to others and yourself is something you would like to stop or reduce and stop, read this article to discover strategies that will help you drink less and leading a healthier life.

## Chapter 4: What, When What, Which, Where

## And Who? What, Why,

"A full bottle was essential. Drinking from half-full bottles was not as relaxing that breaking the seal of the fresh bottle. The peace was in knowing that you had enough ."--Alex North. The Whisper Man

The alcohol-related habits discussed above are the external barriers to reducing or stopping. If you're not able to envision your self quitting drinking There's nothing wrong in that, as long as you are able to keep things in check. If your money is being consumed by alcohol , or you're falling behind on important deadlines or obligations because you drink too often there is something that needs to be changed. The first behavior to look at are those that you can modify by yourself with no external assistance.

The evening hours are generally safe if everyone of your household are properly accounted for and all responsibilities have been fulfilled. This is the place where the quantity of alcohol consumed as well as the time of consumption can be important. If you begin drinking after four or so, and you drink before your children are at home from school, you're losing out on time with them as well as other activities like helping them with their homework , or playing games. If you're regularly buying a huge bottle of dark liquor each once in a while, the quantity you drink could be excessive.

The effects of drinking at night can be easy to hide if you stay at home. Most people don't make an effort to track the amount of alcohol consumed by others without a valid motive to make the effort. There are some signs to look out for. Inconsistent eating or eating in smaller portions of food is common for those who drink. In the end, eating dinner can reduce the amount of calories they absorb from alcohol. They could have breakfast earlier or sleep later, in order to make the most of the time to drink.

Drinkers who drink during the day may perform more efficiently than other drinkers. Because drinking during the day is a time to be social with other people. Drinkers who drink during the day appear as if they've got everything than they do However, this is just part of the routine. They might not be able to remember whom they talk with or what they said. People who decide to take a take a drink during the day are typically doing something completely different and it could be just being on a couch with a friend instead of their own. From concerts to sports events and from beaches to hotels, drinking during the day is typically performed away from home.

Alcoholics always have money to buy liquor and will make the purchase of it a top priority. The majority of functional alcoholics aren't in a position that they can afford to pay bills to buy their drink, however there are exceptions for heavy drinkers. Even when money is scarce the alcoholic will be able to buy whatever they can. A majority of people would rather buy just a single can of 24 ounces of beer instead of going without.

One of the most effective methods to evaluate the way you drink and determine how serious a problem they may be is to look at the quality of your wake-up each day. What is the number of days in the course of a week do you feel feeling hungover? What is the frequency you look at the "hair of your dog" when you wake up? It's common for those drunk to consume similar drinks they had the night before, thinking that it will reduce the severity of the symptoms of a hangover. But the truth is that this is a way to get closer to re-doing the same thing. This practice doesn't offer any time for recovery and only makes the hangovers worse.

A night at home drinking is safe, comparatively speaking and is the preferred choice for certain alcoholics. In the end, drinking in a home environment means you are less at risk of being involved in a crash. Also, it reduces the chance that an alcohol-related drinker will be removed from the road. It is more likely that you will drink out of alcohol at home, rather than refrain from drinking, or ask someone else to help that you stop. Actually this is often the only way to even stop the home-bound alcoholic after they've begun drinking.

A bar is a great place to drink and create a more convivial atmosphere because there are usually more people in the area. Certain bars also offer entertainment for patrons like games tables, or even evenings of karaoke that are specially themed. The greatest risks in this case involve other patrons. In the event of miscommunications, it can lead to drinking disputes, and drinks may be contamination, and everyone needs to get home at the evening. A bar could provide the feeling of being accepted which allows an alcoholic to be a well-known face in a crowd of like-minded people. However, depending on people in the bar you might be disregarded or even yelled at if you announce your desire to cut down.

Drinking Partners

Social drinking is a typical habit in America. If there are people who are aged 18 or older and there are children, it is likely to be alcohol in the event that it is suitable for the surroundings. Work colleagues gather in pubs after working, and people are drinking at festivals or parties and alcohol is likely to be a common sight everywhere there is people. Alcohol, in reality, is a well-known social fluid, which is that is used to relax and get to know each other. Things like bar trivia create a connection between drinking and competition or games at parties such as beer Pong.

A group of people having a get-together to enjoy some drinks and have a chat is a very old idea that was often utilized through Greek philosophers. Studies have shown that people experience reduced inhibitions, less stress and more energy after drinking. This makes it an easy option to relax the tongues and spark conversation. Drinking with friends doesn't require the presence of a large number of people. The first time you meet is in this category.

Social drinking isn't a problem in and of itself. Like all other issues it's a matter of quantities and moderate consumption. Actually the definition of a social drinker can be defined as someone who drinks once or twice every month, but not more than once every week, and who consumes less than three drinks during the time frame. The idea of having a few drinks with a colleague is usually unnoticeable. In the same way, very few people think twice about someone who had one or two drinks in vacation. This is only a problem when binge or heavy drinking alcohol consumption behaviors are evident.

The problem with limiting the amount of alcohol consumed by a person who does not drink by themselves is the added peer pressure. In the end, as many would say drinking one glass of wine never hurts any harm. This is the reason why drinking with friends can result in more frequent drinking. If a person is constantly reaching for a drink whenever one is provided it is possible to not keep track of the amount they've consumed. This type of behavior can cause more serious problems like drinking poisoning or situations of date rape.

In spite of those risks, the act of drinking socially could lead to a change in behaviors. Your acquaintances could be discovering by accident that you can only be with them when you offer alcohol. They may therefore be compelled to ensure that it's available before inviting you. There could be other people in the club who have been alcohol addicts themselves, but aren't prepared to confront the reality of their addiction. Both of these scenarios could create a lot of difficulties for someone trying to reduce their alcohol intake.

It is essential to be open with people who you regularly spend time with, particularly if they accompany you or encourage you to drink. If you'd like to reduce your drinking, establish the limits in a strict manner and stick to the rules. You might decide to treat yourself to a drink at a party after a few hours of sobriety. Make a commitment to yourself. If your friends choose not to listen, then be determined with them. The correct way to phrase things, the safest ways to avoid drinking and observing boundaries will be discussed in greater depth in a subsequent chapter.

If your family members or friends aren't listening and are attempting to bombard you with more drinks in social occasions, you'll must find alternatives. You might need to separate yourself from certain people that are significant to you. It is up to you to determine whether this is a decision you'd like to take swiftly and without fuss or if you'd prefer to explain the situation and allow them to comprehend and accept your new restrictions. The more drastic options might be required to cut down on drinking.

If you are a drinker with your people at work, the solution could be as simple as recommending the possibility of a new spot to meet. Celebrations or events can be enjoyed by drinking alcohol-free drinks and are generally an option in any venue. Bars and restaurants, particularly, are equipped to cater to people who do not drink. Engaging in social settings without alcohol will lessen the need to drink as an ingredient in social lubrication. Begin by chatting with people you feel more comfortable with , and then allow the conversations to flow effortlessly. There's there no requirement to fill each silence or pause. As time passes, you might be able to prove yourself an excellent conversationalist with no drinking.

If you have reduced or stopped drinking completely, social drinking could be a good way to revisit the concept and test your tolerance. It is feasible to take advantage of these types of drinking practices that are safe to allow you to drink alcohol but not lose control completely. Be cautious and honest with yourself when destructive behavior begins to appear once more. Alcoholics who drink heavily might need to quit drinking completely and there's nothing wrong in this. Each person is unique. The most important thing is to have a strong support system around you while you attempt to stay away from alcohol or reduce your intake. The best place to begin searching for this group is to look for those with whom you drink regularly.

There are many reasons to drink.

There are many factors that people could decide to drink. Peer pressure is an important factor. When a person celebrating their birthday or hosting a celebration for friends, the amount of people in the room seems to significantly increase the likelihood there will alcohol available and served. People drink a lot to be a part of the crowd or keep from appearing silly. It is due to the previously mentioned benefits of alcohol as an lubricant for social interactions. While everyone else is being drinking, and enjoying a great time, someone who may not want to drink may be worried about ruining the party and end in drinking.

Social anxiety is a major contributor to social pressure because the desire to conform can cause a person to be more stressed or anxious when they do not seem to fit in. There is a shared experience between those who drink and those with social anxiety disorders. Indeed, people with social anxiety are 20percent more likely to have a problem with alcohol. This typically occurs within 10 years of the diagnosis of anxiety disorder.

Stress is another external cause. Because alcohol sluggishes nerves, alcohol may cause apathy to many emotions. Stressed-out people can be able to relax mentally, emotionally and physically after several drinks. People who drink are more likely to lose things, and this can include details about various stressful events. You shouldn't be stressed out about something you've lost.

Many drink to feel better. The joy and euphoria of numerous drinks is an incentive to make someone who is content to be the center of the celebration. Many people build their entire personality or public image around this concept. Many crazy partygoers do not reveal what transpires when the party's over. Actually, those who drink to feel happy will more often be suffering from depression, and drink alcohol to soothe their depression.

Depression is another reason that people use to drink. Numbing, as mentioned previously, and euphoria could give you a break from depression. Because it isn't generally experienced it is more likely for people to seek the experience to themselves. Drinking alcohol is for feeling good.

There are people who drinkers are an acquired habit. Certain people are in a world of alcohol, alcoholics and alcohol. This makes the more likely they are to drink. Because alcohol was all around it is possible that these individuals will minimize the negative effects and harm alcohol-related harm that many people suffer. A few may be lucky enough to not show any signs of damage and may think that it doesn't apply to them.

The people with addictive personalities are likely to be drinking addicts. People who are addicted to alcohol may begin drinking because of the pressure of peers or exposure to alcohol and any other of the other reasons listed above. They'll keep drinking because they can't stop. A person who is addicted tends to require external stimulation, and will be drawn by the effects of that stimulation. Drugs, alcohol, and other risky behaviors are all natural draw for addicts.

Some people are just drawn to the flavor of certain drinks, however this is a subjective thing and is not the primary motive for someone to turn to drinking alcohol. It is as numerous motivations for drinking as those who drink. A small percentage of alcoholics are able to make drinking routine because they are enjoying life for them. Most of the time, there is a anxiety or stress that helps cause a person to fall into alcoholism slowly. Knowing what the reason for your own addiction to alcohol could be, it will help you get a better handle on getting rid of it.

## Chapter 5: Setting Boundaries

"Meanwhile those 3 a.m. drinkers of this world could lie on their couches struggling to get to sleep, and deserved this rest, if only they could locate it ."--Charles Bukowski

One of the most difficult choices you have to make is to limit your consumption of alcohol. You're committing to quit or at a minimum limit the enjoyment you can get from drinking. You're breaking some of your long-standing routines and you will have to substitute the old habits with something else. If you are unable to find a appropriate replacement, you might go back to drinking alcohol because it's readily accessible. Prior to anything else you should establish limits for yourself and the others who surround you.

The process of establishing these rules with yourself can be more straightforward and may include things such as limit how much cash that you carry to purchase drinks. If this isn't enough, you may want to put your debit or credit card at your home. Maybe you'll limit yourself to one six pack a day as you try to reduce your consumption. Perhaps you'll change your route for home in order to prevent from driving by the local liquor store or bar.

If you're a home drinker, it is possible to take advantage of activities to entertain yourself for a chunk of time that you are normally drinking. If you're away from home and the typical routines of leaving work and going out the door, or eating dinner with your family aren't there, your brain can't instantly switch to the next thought-provoking behavior. It could also expose you to new places, people and events. You might even plan an outdoor dinner once per week with your family or something similar.

Another major issue is others. According to many, the most difficult thing is admitting that you are suffering from problems. In most cases, when someone talks to family members or friends about their addiction to alcohol and their honest feelings are confronted by denial. "You're not all that awful. You don't drink as much. You've never had any issues. You're fine!" These reactions are normal for a variety of reasons.

First, family members and acquaintances of those who abuse alcohol are often unaware of the signs and symptoms until they are living with an alcohol-dependent. Certain functional alcoholics are able to conceal their problems and signs for years , and they are received with astonishment. This is a part of how they deal with the disorder , as and how drinking alcohol is viewed in the society. It is not common for people to think of drinking as dangerous if the individual drinking isn't unsafe. Are you not driving drunk? Absolutely no problem. There's no violence? You're fine.

There are a lot of who will allow alcohol to be a problem in the majority of situations. Everyone drinks. It's such an accepted practice that many who do not live with addiction issues will be unaware about someone who chooses to drink alcohol. However, people who have had to live with addiction sufferers tend to have an anti-drug policy to protect their loved ones. Alcoholics who are in a position to just cut down on their drinking. Others must abstain completely. Family members and friends often follow the example of the addict they have come across.

Whatever the reasons or challenges the alcoholics face, they must be open about their addiction and deal with the issue. The support and care of family and friends can help however, the alcoholics have to establish their own boundaries to reduce their alcohol consumption. This is why establishing limits is crucial. It can be difficult telling your friends and family that you've cut back on your drinking. You must think carefully about what you'll say and be prepared to be extremely confident with the people you have in your life. Being firm could be the most crucial thing to remember, in actual.

People aren't comfortable with creating or observing the boundaries. They simply don't want limits if they are impacted by them. In a way, the same kind of people who may find your boundaries to be absurd or ridiculous are also likely to expect their boundaries to be viewed as almost holy. The double-standard is widespread among those who believe that their boundaries are important to all those who is around them.

The same group of people could overlook your boundaries completely.

It is important to be aware of your limits, what you can accept, and what you will not tolerate. Make these boundaries clear and perhaps even the warning to those who may be pushing your limit. "Hey I've told you I'm not drinking. Do not ask me to drink for another time." After two or three warnings don't be afraid to quit and inform them that this is going to occur. "Listen I've said to that I'm not going take that action. If you try to ask me again, I'm going to leave." After an ultimatum, you must adhere to what you said. Follow through with the consequences you agreed to.

When to establish Boundaries

The process of setting boundaries can be a challenge when people don't adhere to the boundaries. One of the first things you have to be aware of when deciding which boundaries you want to establish is the rights you enjoy. These rights will allow you know whether your boundaries have been violated. They might not be what people think of when it comes to terms of boundaries, but these rights include the freedom to refuse without guilt or feeling guilty, or the right to consider your requirements as important just like everyone else's. This means that these rights are precisely the ones that people often wrestle with when they choose to establish limits.

Boundaries are frequently ignored or by the person who established them, or by others around them when their rights are not respected. Everyone has their own reasons to disregard the boundaries of others. "You helped me the last moment." "It's only this time." "You have done it for somebody other person." "I need it." require to do it." In certain situations it's not really motives but excuses and you'll likely recognize.

It is crucial to pay attention to your body's needs when setting and discussing the specifics of your boundaries with other people. Your body's senses and instinctual reactions will let you know that someone is pushing too over the line and boundaries are required or is being breached. If you get anxious every when someone offers their opinions without soliciting them You must establish some kind of limit with the person. Perhaps they should realize their opinions. The more they share the less likely you will listen.

The boundaries we draw are determined by history and culture, our personal morals as well as life experiences, as well as the way we interact with other people. Understanding when, how and who to establish boundaries that are healthy is essential. The people who drain you or exhaust you might require some limits to place them at a separation from your. Be aware that you're not creating these boundaries in a way to be cruel. It is to protect your physical and mental well-being.

If you are trying to establish boundaries for alcohol, it is possible to go beyond declare that you have quit drinking. You may need to cut down on time spent with old drinking buddies, or separate yourself from those who make you feel stressed. It is also helpful to look for other venues to enjoy your time. Instead of going to the bar visit a park or restaurant. If you're attending a gathering make sure you request a non-alcoholic beverage at the beginning and don't apologize for the need. Set your boundaries clearly regardless of whether you are between you and others.

The process of setting boundaries with other people isn't easy because people do not always pay attention. Equally, it can be difficult to establish limits for yourself due to similar reasons. According to the joke "I made myself an deadline, but I'm sure who made that mistake and he's a fool." Sometimes, however, times, we're more likely to not be listening to our own voices than to listen to other people. The limits we set for ourselves revolve around things such as self-control, and we are able to easily create the excuses of our own.

Healthy boundaries, regardless of who they are can give us to develop and to be vulnerable. If you're sharing too much of your alcohol-related issues for instance, and talking to everyone you meet you might need to set boundaries. If you're not sharing anything or keeping your bad habits to yourself You could adjust the boundaries to allow only a few to be allowed in. The boundaries aren't meant to be unscalable walls that anyone is able to over and are not marks in the sand that allow anyone to jump over.

Saying 'no' is another indicator that you've established a good boundary, and it's both ways. It is acceptable to refuse to do something without guilt, and neither is the person who you're talking to. No one has to be obligated to do anything that causes them feel uncomfortable. Refusal to do something shouldn't cause guilt and should not be the subject of an explanation.

Healthy boundaries aren't designed to exclude anyone for no reason. If you have a friend that you need to avoid spending time with when you are trying to stop drinking, it's due to some reason. Perhaps they are willing to offer you alcohol even though they shouldn't. Perhaps they consume more alcohol than you're comfortable with. No one will be cut off from your life because of a boundary , regardless of any reason you can think of. Anyone who believes they need more details on the reason behind why you have. They don't have to give them a response unless you would like to provide the answer.

How to Keep to Your Boundaries

When making boundaries, it's essential to assert yourself but not aggressive. The boundaries will be firm to other people without individuals feeling angry or that they're being targeted. One method of doing this is through the use of "I declarations." They are used to establish specific boundaries that are non-negotiable without blaming or threats. An example of an statement is "when we go to the bar , and you don't drink, I'm like I'm left out since I'm unable to purchase alcohol. What I want is for us to find a place that does not serve alcohol only at least once or twice every weekly." The boundaries is outlined, along with a rationale and a solution are all covered without making anyone feel uncomfortable about the situation.

I statements are intended to convey thoughts, feelings and opinions without having to think about the thoughts of other people. This is crucial since your personal boundaries are only for only you and no one other. I statements are also a useful method of communicating effectively. Just expressing anger and expressing your emotions about something isn't effective in the long term.

"I do not want to go out to bars anymore" is a true phrase, but not a good one.

The art of saying "no" is another thing to learn when you are trying to maintain limits. Be aware that saying "no" is a complete phrase by itself. There are some who hesitate to state no without additional explanation or information However, that's not necessary in any way. Nobody is obligated to give an explanation for the limits you have set or the reason you have to establish the boundaries.

The setting of boundaries for your belongings and physical space as well as your time is crucial and beneficial when you are trying to cut down on drinking alcohol. For instance, if you purchase a six pack for yourself and restricting yourself to just six drinks, it's completely acceptable to let these beers just to enjoy. It is not required to divulge your information with anyone, or even justify why you're not doing this. Limiting your time can be efficient. You might agree to go out to a bar, but for a minimum of 30 minutes, and you only spend a specific amount on yourself. If you're not purchasing rounds for your friends or taking complimentary drinks from them you are in control of how much you consume.

Other restrictions you could set as you attempt to quit drinking include that you do not have alcohol in your home, aside from the items you buy. It could be decided that having a casual conversation about alcohol isn't allowed. Your friends might be banned or even encouraged, based on what you decide to say, including asking what you've consumed. Encouragement to do this is an opportunity to ensure that you are honest and accountable to your family and friends.

Although setting boundaries isn't often a trend but it is vital for anyone who wants to make their goals be achieved. Without boundaries, you may get dragged into bars or purchasing alcohol as if you'd not ever expressed a desire to make a change. This isn't any good. Setting boundaries that are firm is as important as establishing boundaries. It is also important to establish boundaries for yourself and your family members. Be sure they're not excessive.

One of the most important aspects to set acceptable boundaries is to give your self and others in your vicinity a little amount of grace. You won't be able to leave alcohol without warning or with no reduction. Also, your people who have been drinking with you frequently might need gentle reminders prior to when they decide to stop inviting you to bars every day. Family members who have become accustomed to buying drinks for you might regularly go to the refrigerator. This is what happens. It's just a matter of routine. If you do make these habitual mistakes, when they occur, do not blame yourself, or anyone else who try to assist you.

While doing this it is important to be honest about yourself. There are alcoholics who claim they're trying to reduce their consumption but they make excuses instead of setting the boundaries. "It was a long morning at work." "I'm stressed and want to ease off." "I'll not be able to get through this evening without a drink and a couple." "There was just one bottle left in the bottle." If you're making excuses like these and allowing them to be accepted by yourself consider rephrasing them in I statements to discover the real reason behind them. be.

"Work was stressful and I'd like to unwind by having a drink. ...." "There there was only one more drink left in the bottle and I'm looking for it today because ...." many such excuses later transformed into I statements don't have the best end-of-the-line. It's not the kind of thing you'd like to tell another person if they asked for more details.

Be sure to set boundaries that are in line with your objectives. Do not create boundaries that are unnecessary or ones that don't actually assist you. Your boundaries, just as your goals, have to be clear, quantifiable realistic, achievable, and time-bound. "I will not drink more that one six-pack the next evening." This limit is specific to the following night, and is measurable in terms of the amount of alcohol you're restricting you to. This something you will surely be successful by focusing on self-discipline.

When you set goals and limits be sure that you're surround yourself with people who are supportive of you. There are likely to be relatives or friends who are thrilled to learn about your efforts to reduce your drinking, and eager to hear about any updates you provide throughout the process. It's also possible that you have people who been struggling with their drinking behaviors. If this is the scenario, there's an established support system to call upon in times of need. It is important to ensure that those whom you have around you be supportive of your efforts to reduce your drinking. It's never too early to know that an small gesture of kindness or a sympathetic ear can be all it takes to make a difference.

## Chapter 6: Requires Regulating And Replacing

"Alcohol is the sole substance in the world that, once you stop taking it, you're seen as suffering from a disease ."--Holly Whitaker"Quit Like a Woman: The Uncompromising Choice to Avoid Drinking in a Society Obsessed with Alcohol

If you've decided to decrease the alcohol consumption it is recommended to begin immediately. In the event that you drink less, that you consume lesser calories, which will result in better overall health. Also, you will need to replenish the calories which was used to calculate the amount of alcohol you consume. This is when you should choose wiser choices: Juice, water and more healthy drinks, and healthier food items. Juice in particular, must be considered as a an element of cutting down on alcohol.

The issue of replacing calories could be difficult, particularly when cutting down on alcohol may result in cravings for sugar. The reason why you feel this way lies in the fact that sugar just like alcohol causes an increase in dopamine as well as serotonin from the brain. These chemicals that make you feel good are the reason alcohol is believed to be addicting. The replacement of one substance by another in the interest of producing specific brain chemicals is referred to as addiction transfer. But with regards to the replacement of sugar and alcohol it is just the beginning of a problem that may be brewing.

More than 95% of ex- drinkers suffer from hypoglycemia, or low blood sugar. The sugar glucose, which is a basic one within your bloodstream, functions as the brain's fuel and brain, therefore when it's low, it's difficult to perform well. Limiting alcohol intake decreases the amount of glucose that your body gets from. This could lead to anxiety, confusion, and stress.

A craving for sugar as you try to reduce or stop drinking the habit of drinking is normal, and is not something you should attempt to avoid. Your body is trying to keep the blood sugar levels it's used to, and the brain is not getting enough the chemicals that make you feel good, due to the lesser amount of alcohol that you're taking in. It's not a matter about willpower, it's the body begging for the things it requires. Therefore, don't resist it. If you're looking for some extra snacks or desserts to last several evenings rather than going out for a drink It's fine.

There are people who find themselves feeling guilty when they reach for sugar to substitute to treat an addiction to alcohol. There are many methods to help ease the sugar cravings and eat in regular intervals. When you are in the beginning stages of sobriety not eating meals, or putting off eating for too long consume food can cause you to crave more since your body's requirement for calories increases. It is important to plan for eating something every 4 hours or less, and snacking between meals. Make sure you are focusing on protein, fat and fiber instead of simply carbs. The only thing carbs can do is convert into simple sugar which puts your body in the exact spot that you're currently in.

Protein is crucial, especially in breakfast, which tends to be a heavy carbohydrate meal. Carbs, like sugar, can trigger energy drops since your body will deplete its stores of fuel faster. Also, include peanut butter on your toast, or cook an additional egg. Protein, healthy fat and fiber help to ensure that your blood sugar levels remain in check. These nutrients also provide your body with the nutrients that it requires to start recovering from the alcohol you've consumed. High-protein snacks are also beneficial during the middle of the day when your energy levels naturally decrease.

When you think about what kinds of foods you indulge in, the amount and times, and also the amount of alcohol you're planning to replace, it's crucial to prepare for this drop in energy. Complex carbohydrates and alcohol both are easy to pick up whenever you feel hungry and can be very effective in warding away cravings, but they can just lead to an increase in the problems you're currently experiencing. You should opt for fresh fruits. Hard-boiled eggs and nuts are another good snack that you can grab and go.

If you have difficulty or aren't able to get rid of the entire amount of calories that you take in by drinking there are other measures you can take to reduce the amount of alcohol you're taking in. A lower alcohol consumption is a simple solution however, many struggle with this concept. The entire idea of controlling drinking alcohol is often ridiculed or dismissed, especially in the male population. It is believed that men can drink a glass of beer to get away from whatever the issue might be. This is so popular that some men are mocked when they announce their plans to stop drinking. If you choose not to make cutting back a public announcement however, there are still options to cut down on calories or sugar as well as alcohol.

You can purchase smaller quantities of alcohol to limit the amount of alcohol you consume. The switch to a light drink or another lighter type of alcohol may also affect the amount of calories you consume. Eat food every time you drink, and don't put off adding glasses or pitchers of water to help keep you well-hydrated while drinking. These small adjustments need a change in consciousness, and a little amount of extra attention.

If you purchase your own alcohol from an upscale grocery store instead of drinking at a bar, be sure to track the alcohol content of the drink, as well as the calories. Anything that has 20 percent ABV or alcohol per liter (ABV) is more than a beverage that is at 8% ABV. This measurement indicates the amount of alcohol contained in the whole container. For example, a 15-ounce bottle at 3.3% ABV is 45 percent alcohol.

In some bars, you might be able to request drinks that are lighter and don't contain a large amount of alcohol. White wines, light beers and singles that are doubles over mixed drinks are a few methods to cut down your consumption of alcohol. Smaller portions and containers are also great ways to reduce the amount you consume. These are steps that may be simpler to follow than doing every time you do math.

It is also crucial not to be lured by sales or discounts. Do not purchase a larger quantity of alcohol due to sales. If six packs are available for purchase one, get one half price and you've only planned to purchase one, stay with the strategy. The cost of buying more is not always the bargain that the public portrays it to be, regardless of what you're purchasing. You are purchasing more than you had originally had in mind.

If you're at an establishment or bar there is a need to be attentive to the bartenders or waiters in the vicinity. If you are not careful, an employee who is too enthusiastic could pour you more drinks than you'd like to drink. This is not a deliberate act by them however it could put your in the same situation regardless of the motives. A lot of drinkers drink too quickly even though tiny doses of alcohol over time can increase their BAC.

The idea of practicing awareness is exactly the reason it is important to be aware of the limits you're setting for yourself. If you don't know the exact location of the finish line then how do you be able to tell when you've crossed it? That is without a set of limits beforehand How do you know when to stop? Setting these limits may be difficult because there are people who like to push the limits. This is the reason you need to set solid boundaries with yourself and your coworkers.

One common recommendation for those who find themselves in this position is to ensure that there is all alcohol out of the house. This is where the help of family and friends can be indispensable. If the people closest to you are aware that you're trying to reduce your consumption, they may be willing assist by adhering to the limits you've set. For instance, you could opt to only purchase alcohol in a certain amount on certain days of the week , as instead of every night. If you are required to keep alcohol in your home, the limits are essential. A six-pack, three nights per week could be acceptable but it has to be kept up.

Avoiding alcohol in the home However, it is a way to reduce how much temptation a person is exposed to when trying to limit. It is harder to avoid when it's physical. For example, the desire to go out to drink an alcohol boost is something that could be ignored or put away. If it's at the end of the hall sitting in cold and waiting, refusing is much more difficult.

Set goals that are specific to you will help you celebrate more often when you've achieved the goals. This will allow you to be more aware of any challenges you encountered when trying to achieve the objective. It is important to keep in mind that goals are not an end all be all every deadline. If your goal doesn't get initially met, then alter your goal to meet your goal.

The goal of drinking just one six-pack per day may be too much, based on your usual consumption. It is possible for you to state "I had been drinking between 10 and 12 drinks per night. I'm planning to reduce that to 8 drinks per night for this next period of time." It's still cutting back, but not enough that it becomes impossible. If you fail in the beginning, it doesn't mean you're likely to fail. Re-evaluate your goals and make adjustments. Perhaps instead of going to bed every night it is possible to try every each night. Another important aspect to consider in these flexible objectives is not to utilize attainability as an excuse to indulge. A reduction in your intake of three nights every week doesn't necessarily mean that you indulge in more drinks on other nights to make up for the time you didn't get to. The aim is to reduce. It's not good in the long term if you reduce your intake to six packs on a weekday, only to purchase 30 packs on the weekends.

Alcohol Withdrawal

If you're trying to reduce your alcohol consumption, it's an ideal idea to record your progress. This allows for archival purposes as well as an account in writing to see your progress in time. It is possible to track your progress your progress in a journal or an Excel spreadsheet on your computer. You can also take quick notes on your mobile phone. Things to track include the amount you're drinking, the kind of alcohol you are drinking, the time and where you drink it, as well as your mood. You might also want to write any signs down.

The signs of cutting back on alcohol, similar to the symptoms triggered by heavy drinking, could be physical, mental or emotional. These symptoms may also be experienced by people who are cutting down on their alcohol consumption or abstain from drinking completely. Individuals who plan to stop drinking for good tend to have more severe symptoms, however it doesn't mean there aren't any other individuals who suffer. The withdrawal symptoms begin to manifest within a couple of hours after drinking the last one. They begin as simple symptoms of a hangover, but could become more severe according to how much the person drank.

Since alcohol can slow the brain it releases more chemicals in order to offset the negative effects. The extra chemicals are more abundant than those who don't drink. This is because the brain's normal the production of additional chemicals is not stopped just because alcohol is in smaller quantities. The chemicals that are added are present and can put the person who is drinking to a state of hyperstimulation. It lasts less than a few days but it is still painful.

The feeling of fatigue, irritation and feelings of jitteriness or nervousness are some indicators of withdrawal from alcohol. However, these symptoms can also be due to the effects of a hangover. The presence of stimulant chemicals can make noises seem excessively loud, and lights too bright. In combination with the difficulty in thinking clearly and a heightened stimulation of the senses can be combined with a confused mind and can cause intense mood fluctuations. The stress, fatigue and sudden bursts that are energy-rich are the result of simple sugars that are absent from the blood. Because sugars can be the main source of fuel for the body, depleting them may cause physical signs and symptoms.

Skin that is clammy, high blood pressure and headaches are the beginning of what's to come as your body is able to process the last drop of alcohol. No more is expected. Hand tremors, sweating and paleness are all easy indicators for those suffering from withdrawal. Vomiting and insomnia are two signs that frequently hinder people from cutting down. They'd rather battle hangovers and put their bodies at risk rather than suffer withdrawal. The withdrawal symptoms are the most common cause of the relapse as well. Some people reach for an alcohol drink to make withdrawal symptoms disappear. This can trigger the whole cycle over.

Another, more severe type of withdrawal that is typically only observed in extremely severe alcohol users. It is known as delirium Tremens. Those suffering from it often suffer from malnutrition before symptoms begin to set in. About one out of 20 people who suffer from the disorder is likely to die from the. This type of extreme withdrawal from alcohol requires medical attention until symptoms subside. Tremors, hallucinations, fever and seizures are a few frequent signs that someone is suffering from delirium tremens.

While severe withdrawal symptoms can persist for longer, like for the delirium tremens syndrome, there's also a standard timeline for typical withdrawal symptoms. The symptoms can begin anywhere between four and twelve hours after the last drink. The symptoms can be felt by those who have been influenced by alcohol, regardless of whether they're trying to reduce their consumption or deciding to quit altogether. The most significant difference lies in the intensity of the symptoms that the sufferers feel.

Acute withdrawal from alcohol tends to be the most severe within two days of quitting, with symptoms beginning to improve around the fifth day. They include insomnia, restlessness or irritability, mood swings and difficulty eating. Certain minor symptoms, like insomnia or anxiety can be present but at a lesser intensity for as long as six months. Extreme symptoms, like hand tremors or fainting, or sweating, can cause delirium tremens. The symptoms of delirium can manifest within the initial four days after stopping drinking, but it can be delayed for up to 10 days before it manifests. The symptoms that are severe may last for up to five days.

The withdrawal symptoms are unpleasant at best and can have an impact on anyone who is near to the person experiencing these withdrawal symptoms. It can be a difficult time for all concerned however, it is just temporary in the long term. Don't let a few weeks of discomfort keep you from doing the things you need to take care of yourself and the people you love. Drinking plenty of water, keeping your the sugar levels high and giving yourself the opportunity to forgive yourself can all help to ease withdrawal symptoms and make life simpler overall. You can go through withdrawal with ease and get to the other side of the fence where you can consider alternatives for recovery.

Why is it important to regulate and replace

If you're drinking a 30-pack every weekend or you are drinking a 12 pack every night, the choice to cut down on drinking may mean that the alcohol has more influence over your life than you would like. If this is the situation the mere fact that you're trying to reduce your intake isn't enough. It is necessary to alter the amount you drink to reduce the amount. Making this change will allow you to feel more confident about yourself and about your decision. In addition, drinking less alcohol will result in a savings of money that isn't devoted to alcohol. The savings added by these extra drinks can be very significant over time.

Limiting the amount you drink does not only provide evidence of your progress, but also it also ensures you are at the helm of your lifestyle. The decision you make your own of the amount you're able to drink gives some control to you. The decision to set these limits for yourself is not just about cutting back. It shows you are still a participant on the wheel metaphorically. You make the choices on your own.

The careful management of alcohol intake could also affect the way withdrawal symptoms manifest and the severity of them. If you limit your consumption with a an organized approach and be patient to do it, you increase the chances of being successful. Your tolerance will not be restored in the event that your food intake isn't the same. This means that the overall condition of your body will increase and your body will begin to recover. If however you revert back to previous habits, you are doing yourself no favors and could cause more harm than they were prior to. If someone is cut back but then relapses back to drinking in a hurry it is likely that they'll be back to their normal levels easily. This can result in becoming more drunk and staying there for longer.

The replacement of routine behaviors such as drinking, and any other routines or habits that are tied to it is a further step to guarantee your success. Instead of going to the bar and search for an alcohol-free drink You could suggest a different place to limit the temptation to drink. It is possible to use excuses when people are urging the need to consume alcohol. It's a good excuse to start your day early and medication that reacts badly when mixed with alcohol or even being designated driver are all excuses that aren't likely to raise any questions or concerns. You may also choose to serve as the designated driver, rather than using it as an excuse. This allows you to enjoy time with your friends and feel secure knowing that everyone with you will be in safety, no matter the amount of alcohol they consumed.

The emergence of new routines and habits is designed to break out of the cycle that you may have created. Going somewhere else than the bar could keep you from the temptation. Cash isn't as important and having no checks or cards will restrict the amount of alcohol you are able to purchase. A designated driver can end the issue completely for nights when you decide to go this route. If your typical group of friends is always drinking it might be a good idea to have a relaxing time with family instead. Your kids or partner will likely enjoy the time together. Watching you completely sober, engaging in a relaxed manner, could provide a glimpse into your goal that you're striving towards and the future that you could be able to share.

Changes in habits and behavior could include some odd ones such as paying for gas at the pump, instead of going to the store. You could buy soda at the same time you used to buy beer, thus substituting the sugars aswell as satisfying your psychological desire for drinking a cold beverage. If the alcohol you prefer is always served in a particular glass at home, think about eliminating the glass. If your alcohol drinks are always served with straws or ice and straw, you could consider removing them for a short time to prevent your mind from thinking that you are drinking alcohol when there's none. If you are looking for the taste of a mixer drink but not the alcohol, you can look into buying mixers that are alcohol-free and drinking them straight.

You may be looking for new ways to fill your time that aren't you've been drinking. If you love watching sporting events, not drinking a drink in the middle of the night can make you feel like you're missing something, regardless of whether you're watching live or telecast. Engaging in exercise or sports can give a sense of competitiveness and excitement to your daily life, which could provide a replacement for some of the pleasure that you felt when you opened a bottle of wine. Participating in sports that are competitive or exercise will also improve the overall health of your body. Outdoor activities when the weather permits it will provide you with more sunlight and fresh air. This can boost your overall health.

This is a great opportunity to enhance your skills through a variety ways. Perhaps you'd like to master something new. Building shelves, or creating a book -- there's an abundance of options that are available. If you're looking to make use of the your time with alcohol and smoking, it's wiser in the long run to learn a new skills or knowledge. You can try your own new art form or learn how to dance. Some of these ideas could aid in meeting new people and enjoy time at other places than the local bar, thus separating you from the routine and vice versa.

Whatever you decide to do to spend your time doing or substitute your drinking with you will surely some benefits that can be derived. Reduced drinking, and making new friends , or developing new skills simultaneously is a wonderful idea. When you determine what behavior and interests you wish to do apart from drinking, you will be able to create a new group of friends or maybe be reintroduced back to the one you have been with for a while. People behave differently when drinking. If you can convince your acquaintances to join you in activities that aren't drinking and reconnect with them as friends who aren't drinking. This will strengthen your friendships and let you know people who could be there with after you've stopped being as of drinking.

The new habits you develop and the stricter restrictions regarding your drinking habits will help you cut down on your alcohol consumption. Explore new places and people to hang out with, should you choose. In locations where alcohol isn't permitted could give you an increased appreciation of entertainment venues that you've never considered. Don't be afraid to take advantage of the time normally consumed by drinking, and do whatever you can to avoid traditional routines from dominating. It is possible to learn new card games or revive an old-fashioned love of reading. There's no limit to what you can do! The search for new interests can lead to new abilities or new skills and new companions. Over time, it might uncover a new you too.

## Chapter 7: Getting Assistance

"When you're young, you drink to be social however, when you're older drinking, you're not sociable. ."--Robert Black

An addict who is recovering can look for various ways to receive assistance. In the end, many of us are not able to go by ourselves when addiction is involved. There's nothing wrong with seeking assistance, but what can you request in this instance? One of the first things that people do is talk to their physicians. This is logical, given the impact alcohol can have on your body. When you speak to your doctor, as when you first looked into your behavior for yourself You must be sincere. Don't sensationalize, but don't lie either. If you're regularly drinking 10 standard drinks per evening, you should inform your physician that.

Your doctor will likely ask you a variety of questions regarding your drinking habits. They may also need to speak with relatives or friends to obtain the full understanding of the current situation you're in. But this cannot be done without your consent and the people that whom the doctor consults with will not have access to personal details regarding your drinking habits. An examination will be conducted to ensure that you are assessed for any damages resulted from your drinking. Imaging tests and lab tests are also typical. They will require x-rays or ultrasounds, as well as blood draw. They will also look for signs of damage.

There aren't any specific tests for alcohol dependence however, certain common signs and symptoms may indicate the condition. This includes things like liver damage, irregular blood sugar levels, and an abnormal blood pressure, among others. All of these symptoms are an effect of alcohol's effect on the body as explained in chapter 1. These symptoms, like organ damage, don't disappear in a flash. They'll be on the table for your doctor's attention for up to a week following an intense drinking session according to the symptoms your doctor is trying to find.

Many medical interventions can be considered to aid those looking to reduce their drinking. A stay in the hospital is most likely to occur in extreme cases when the individual's drinking poses an a danger to them or other people. It is usually the case that the patient will be being in the hospital for a period of time while they cleanse their drinking. Detoxification is a term used for a medically-supervised withdrawal. Sedating drugs can be administered to ease effects of withdrawal.

Psychological counseling can be used to provide both outpatient and inpatient treatment. This could involve things such as confronting the realities of drinking and the destruction that went along from it, as well in establishing concrete plans to change the direction of your life. These plans can include getting new skills or establishing an action plan for treatment. Goal setting, self-help guides and methods for changing behavior are all commonplace, and so is regular counseling when the patient is experiencing difficulties.

There are various medications that are injectable and oral available to block the positive effects of alcohol or intensify the bad feelings. If you're on one of these medicines and decide to take a drink, you could be suffering from nausea, severe vomiting and headaches due to. It's similar to having hangovers without drinking. Many people, including non-alcoholics will agree that it removes a lot of enjoyment out of the experience.

Other treatment options for alcoholism also include measures to stop damage or further harm on the body. The follow-up treatment focuses on support, typically through counseling. Other psychological issues can also be treated because they are typically related to alcohol dependence. They include depression and anxiety. They generally can be treated through psychotherapy and medication.

The concept of following-up treatment and assistance is an accepted practice within recovery circles. Once any medical treatment has been completed, most sufferers are left with cravings or perhaps mild withdrawal symptoms and no idea of what to do following that. There are options at this point, which include group therapy, like Alcoholics Anonymous and private therapy, as well as various treatment options for behavioral issues. Each is a good option, with advantages and disadvantages, as well as a the rate of success.

Recovery from alcohol regardless of the methodused, has a very high rate of relapse. Ninety percent of those who drink will have some form of relapse within the first four years of recovery. Relapses can be caused through anything from beer ad at the side of the road, to an extreme stress period within the life of an alcoholic. The cause isn't so important, but the way the alcoholic deals with it. Other triggers that are common are depression and isolation and both can occur as a consequence of an alcoholic's decision to stop.

Former drinking companions might not be interested in seeking them out. With no social lubricant from alcohol, those who have been drinking might find that they're not able to socialize. Whatever the reason an alcoholic seeking help should be conscious of their behavior in order to avoid falling back into the old habits. Although alcohol might not be prevalent or encouraged, an individual is only able to get from therapy what they're willing to invest in it.

Refraining from sharing or expressing themselves, and ending therapy early are excellent examples of how you can't get the most benefit from therapy. Anyone who plays an active part during their journey to recovery, and is involved in the support group or discovers an alternative way to talk about and securely discuss the difficulties of cutting down on drinking more often will quit drinking rather than leave.

Different types of recovery therapy

Talk therapy, or psychotherapy is the most commonly used non-medical treatment for alcohol dependence. It is a common practice in support groups or 12-step programs, in individual counseling and similar. It is believed that sharing stories of struggles of symptoms, struggles and triumphs may give an impression of belonging and also reassurance. In the end, if a person with a bad habit is able to reduce their drinking to be able to find an offer for a new job and get a new job, nothing can stop you. These strategies rely on mutual support and shared experiences to keep people engaged in their recovering. It's much easier to confess to some of the most painful withdrawal symptoms from alcohol such as stomach problems, if you are aware that the people you share with have experienced the same issues.

Psychotherapy is a practice that can be conducted in a group or one-on-one. This type of therapy typically goes deep into any experience or abuse that could have led to the development of harmful behavior, such as alcoholism. It could include methods like cognitive behavior therapy. This helps the therapist and the patient to change the way they think to help them better manage and face life's challenges. This type of therapy that is goal-oriented involves expressing the emotions of one's life and developing resilience and assertiveness.

Dialectical Behavior Therapy (DBT) is another option one could pick. It teaches behavior skills, including mindfulness, which is being completely present at the moment. It is usually achieved by only focusing on breathing. Emotional regulation, which is a different course in DBT will teach you how to deal with and respond to extreme emotions whenever they arise. It is usually about reducing an emotion or considering problems with a relaxed, rational mental attitude. Accepting negative emotions instead of leaving them behind, also known as distress tolerance is an approach that is often favored by alcohol addicts. Personal effectiveness is the final essential aspect of DBT which is when the person concentrates on themselves and their needs instead of being concerned about other people in their lives.

If talking about your problems is not your thing, you could be helped by an experiential therapy. It involves looking into the unconscious and connecting with the feelings of one's self. These are ones that appear most like traditional therapies. Music therapy, art therapy and the equine therapy are among the most popular treatments that involve an experiential approach. On the surface these methods appear to help patients talk about their issues by first relaxing and then not thinking about the issues.

The family therapy approach draws other people in to help the therapist understand more about the person. It can be a good way to identify what behavior might be affecting family members and friends of the person who is alcoholic, as well as the issues that may require attention. Problems with anger or poor management of finances may only be noticed by the spouse of the alcoholic for instance. The therapist who is involved in family therapy cases will collaborate with the whole group to address all the needs of everyone as the addict recovers. This includes educating about the addiction model, as well as providing coping strategies to all members of the group.

There are a variety of therapies and types that help addicts manage and get over their addiction. One of the most well-known is the 12-step facilitation therapy. It is designed to complement 12-step rehabilitation groups like Alcoholics Anonymous. The principal principles of this group include acceptance of the model of addiction as a disease and active participation in group sessions, and the acceptance of an inner power while adhering to the recovery process.

The options are nearly as diverse in terms of forms of treatment that could be offered that there's people looking for it, however the 12-step program may be the most popular and well-known regarding the control of addiction. These organizations tend to be self-directed and religiously oriented but they are also non-denominational, non-political and non-. The main focus is on the infamous 12 steps to guide addicts to recovery. The steps can be repeated as necessary and performed in the order that is most beneficial for the addict who is who is working on them.

The 12 steps contain the possibility of admitting wrongdoing apologize, taking responsibility for the actions. Following that, individuals are encouraged to conduct an analysis of themselves to find any other illegal act or injury they have caused to another. Following a sincere apology and some form of restitution, it is the expectation that there will be some form or spiritual realignment. A person who is addicted is to become an advocate of the 12-step plan and share it with others about it. They should also turn away from the habit which caused such pain throughout their life.

Whatever type of recovery or therapy may be the best fit for you, it's recommended to include others who can support you to help you cut back on alcohol. By bringing in other people, you will have an opportunity to share your experiences with people who may be able to relate to the issues. Therapists who are licensed are required to keep their sessions private. Friends may be asked to show the same respect in the event that you would like. Therapy is often viewed as a negative thing within many circles however being honest and open about your issues can help you discover patterns and connections that might need to be altered.

Assistance Outside of Therapy

Certain people aren't ready to express their feelings to a therapist , or to a trusted friend. They might want to tackle issues by themselves, as having others involved hasn't assisted before or resulted in worse problems. Perhaps they do not have insurance that covers the cost for therapy. Whatever the reason there are non-medical and non-therapy options that can help alleviate the burdens of addiction and recovery.

Certain of them are based on simple lifestyles, while others promote an alteration in the attitude of addicts.

Regular exercise is a popular choice for many. This could help alleviate some physical signs of addiction, as well as cleansing. The beginning of a routine exercise program can provide a way to stay away from the urge to drink. The endorphins, along with other positive chemicals which flood the brain after an exercise routine could, in time, substitute the buzz from alcohol. Since exercise can lead to losing weight, improved health and increased energy The person who drinks will get more compliments from the people in their vicinity. This is a further incentive to reduce alcohol consumption since it is believed to trigger weight growth. Be sure to keep it in moderation. There's no reason to be hooked on fitness after you have let the alcohol go.

Some people are inclined to record the amount of alcohol they drink. It can be a method to be accountable. Recording the amount you drink as well as how you feel and what could happen due to your drinking creates a concrete record.

Looking back on these notes could help you remember why you decided to end your drinking. You should keep track of the effects of alcohol, hangovers, or any other issue that could arise. These could range from minor incidents like tripping on furniture to more serious issues like fights at bars or sexual assault.

Relaxation techniques can be a great way to distract yourself when an alcoholic is attracted to drink. These typically include deep breathing or shifting the focus of the mind to a particular area or body part. Utilizing these strategies can help the alcoholic to calm down after having was tempted to drink to calm their anger. The process of getting rid of stress through relaxing your muscles in the body can prevent actions or habits that revolve on the tension experienced when someone is angry. Relaxing the tension can alleviate the mood and reduce the need to drink alcohol.

Making positive changes and altering one's mindset requires deliberate effort and lots of awareness. However, it is possible to change triggers that might already be identified. If an addict has a family member who is a source of frustration or one that "drives the person to drink" it is ideal situation to change their mental attitude. Perhaps this person is excited about life, and eager to share that happiness with those in their life. It's an alteration in attitude that takes some time to establish and longer for acceptance, however it's possible to achieve. A positive outlook could eliminate the need to drink if you are depressed or sad also.

The ability to let off the future can tie to mindfulness, which is discussed in the earlier chapters of the book. The ability of an alcohol user to let go of circumstances they are not in control of requires effort, but it can be a way to eliminate triggers for certain. A lot of people drink due to their anxiety about the future. What will be the next pay day? What's your next dinner? The idea of leaving the future behind is not a complete indecisiveness and lack of plan ahead. Instead, it indicates the absence of overplanning. The only things we can take control of in this world is our own. Trying to control anything over anything else isn't always useful in the long run.

When we let these worries go instead of dwelling on the issue, addicts may be able to stop drinking and have a better satisfaction in their lives.

Whichever method of recovery you pick take care to allow yourself to grow now. If one method isn't effective, try a different one. Perhaps you require counseling with your partner in the family exercising with a sibling, or cognitive behavior therapy by yourself to see if things are working. There's no one size for all, and there is no one approach that can assist everyone to reduce their drinking. Find out what works for you, and tweak to what doesn't. Be patient and allow yourself the time to adapt to new circumstances before you decide to abandon any method or learning. If you really want to limit your alcohol consumption, even if it's just a tiny amount, you'll be successful over time.

**Chapter 8: Recovery And A Path Moving Forward**

"Those who deny reality should not be able to advise others about the nature of reality or what it will be done in the face of ."--Daniel Chappell. Chappell

Whatever the reason why you decided to drink or to stop to a certain extent, taking a review of the impact of alcohol on your life could reveal certain unpleasant facts. There may be family members or friends asking to quit. Your bank account could have a shockingly low balance. Perhaps you're doing well and have garbage cans stuffed with trash that serve as reminders to your addiction. Whatever the reason, once you've found the path towards recovery, be aware that it's a long process.

Relapses are common among recovering alcohol users. In fact, they happen for 90% of the people within the first four years after stopping. In addition, withdrawal-related symptoms and the relapse aren't only experienced by those who are not abstinence-based or avoiding alcohol, either.

Anyone who is restricting their intake may experience these symptoms. If withdrawal symptoms arise then treat them in the best way you can. If you have the same symptoms again Don't get yourself into a rage for it.

Although the above statistic may sound frightening, as if that odds are stacked against you, it's not the situation. First year of recovery is by far the toughest, with a 30 percent relapse rate. In the second year of sobriety 21 percent of recovering alcohol addicts had at the very least one recrudescence. In three years, the percentage is reduced to just a few digits. Relapses are inevitable and all you have to be doing is acknowledge the fact that they will happen and then get over them and move ahead.

Begin each day at a time and then a week at an time. If you're experiencing setbacks, keep in mind that tomorrow is a new day. One setback isn't going to ruin the work you've put into it. You'll always have an opportunity to start again waiting for you at the next dawn. Of obviously this is a notion that many struggle with. They might not be accustomed to forgive themselves or treat themselves with compassion.

If you're recovering from alcohol dependence It may be helpful to imagine yourself as having a long-term health problem. Diabetes sufferers must pay attention to what they consume. Similar to that, you need to stay away from factors that could cause you to consume more alcohol. This is why setting limitations can be helpful. If you are able to drink the specified amount of alcohol or spend a set quantity of money you'll be more in control of the circumstance. It is unlikely that you will be intoxicated to the point of despair. You won't be tempted to revert back to old habits or bad habits.

If you've followed the advice contained in this book, you've likely found a few activities to take the place of time previously filled with drinking. It is okay to discuss these activities with your family or friends if you'd like. They may join you, rather than pushing you to the limit. Your recovery may open the door to more and a more supportive group with your family members and close friends. Although this might be an idealistic idea, you'll never know if you do not take a shot.

The process of cutting down on alcohol may be a more difficult task than abstinence completely because it is possible to drink. It is still possible to drink with a set limit. It's an easy excuse to drink more than what your limits allow however, that's the addiction talking. These excuses could actually be component of your addiction patterns. This could be due to old habits returning and causing you to fall into further troubles. Beware of allowing this to occur.

By identifying your triggers, you can choose to be able to avoid them completely or completely alter your thoughts about them. If you decide to drive down another street in order to avoid crossing the bar, you could locate something else on that street that you are interested in. If you buy your beer regularly at the same place check to see if they offer other items. This option may not work suitable for everyone as it isn't a way to limit the possibility of exposing yourself to old locations, old habits or even flings. If you want to stay clear of the triggers that trigger you then that's fine and is usually figured out.

If you're making the attempt to heal from addiction to alcohol, you have to ensure that there is a network of support there. Find a group of people who are supportive of your efforts and ensure that you are successful. Perhaps you can arrange for rides to and from therapy session or group of support. This type of gesture could aid you by making sure you are on time and don't need to worry about the temptation of driving due to the bar or another cause.

Keep in mind that relatives and friends of someone suffering from alcohol-related disorders have identical rights addict. They also have the ability to set guidelines and limits on the amount they spend or do not provide assistance for the addict. One spouse might refuse to contact them to help on "sick days" in the event that their spouse is still recovering from an alcohol-related hangover. They might be hesitant to go on a beer run even for the tiny amount that recovering alcohol addicts are accepting. Certain individuals can request not to call after dark or at unorthodox time. It's all fine.

If you are trying to cut back on their alcohol consumption must ensure that they have a solid back-up system. This includes those who accept calls at odd times or for a variety of strange reasons. An addict recovering from alcohol may need to request for support around two in the morning, if they're frightened at the prospect of taking drinks and are attempting to avoid it. In such a case it is crucial to remind the person who is alcoholic of the reason they chose to reduce or stop drinking.

This is an essential element to changing the way an alcoholic's thoughts. If there are significant goals that are in place that could be more easily achieved with alcohol-free life, these goals have to be considered whenever feasible. Apart from improving your health, perhaps you are looking to reduce your expenses by not purchasing alcohol. This goal could be further emphasized by allocating the money to something. You can save money for an excursion or even a new car, maybe. There are a variety of alternatives for this, as well as an array of goals that you can used to motivate you.

If the motivation for this isn't enough , or somebody has a different view then the emphasis may need to change. Certain people are attracted by the prospect of an award. Others are attracted due to the fear of failing. If you're one of them it is better to make a list of pros and cons made. It can be used to compare the benefits that alcohol can bring to an individual's life with the benefits they can achieve if they stop drinking. It is likely that cutting down to alcohol consumption will do more benefits than continuing drink.

If you take the right steps and treatment taken in advance anyone trying to get back to normal from addiction can achieve the success they desire. It requires patience and an knowledge of your own addiction. It is important to understand the triggers that cause you anxiety, what can be done to prevent it and what you can change as well as what the unwelcome behavior will be replaced with. You can establish an appropriate support system. Therapy from a professional is accessible to those who gain from it. Whatever you have to accomplish, if you are willing to do the effort, you'll be successful.

Everything changes

Knowing the reason you wish to limit your drinking is an important element to achieve success. Another important factor is knowing how can cut down. Avoidance, reframing thoughts and recognizing triggers are all dealt with however there are some who require more. It is not possible to spend all of your time in an online support group. Some people may be more beneficial to take an end of the group. But what's the reason?

A few alcoholics who struggle to achieve success may need to employ more extreme methods. Many have different views of their addiction, themselves and the world surrounding them. This worldview distortion is the result of an all-or-nothing mentality. Everything is taken to the extreme in the world of an alcoholic. There is no moderate and no middle ground and there isn't a gray area. The existence of extremes can result in further instances of the similar.

A new beginning is the ideal solution for people who wish to stop drinking. This implies cutting off any ties to previous behaviors and habits, locations, and even individuals. The new surroundings may not be able to eliminate every trigger however, it will at most eliminate the familiarity of the old routines. You don't have to worry about those you used to dine and drink with if they're not a part of your daily life. Being far from the bar can make it difficult to get to it often.

The idea behind this method is to create a refining oneself. It is possible for people to completely change their life, but these types of methods that are extreme can be the most effective method to shift your thoughts and habits. If you're unable to leave your job, you may be able to relocate. If you aren't able to relocate, you could modify your driving route. If you aren't able to do that then you might need to get involved with your support group. For a couple of days, you could carry cash to pay for lunch at the office or to fill up your vehicle. When your cash is located at your home or in the possession of a family member or person, it's not possible to drink more alcohol.

If you decide to push yourself to the limit to reinvent your self, it could be better to go to the maximum extent you are able to. If a friend you haven't met in a while and doesn't know about your past suggests a visit to a bar it is possible to say that you're not drinking. If they insist the issue, you can say that your medication won't let the. This prevents you from looking deep into your past and gives you a common reason. This could result in a new location or grant you the responsibility of the designated driver. Whatever the case, you're likely not to have to be worried about the getting caught up in the flurry of.

Talking to people you meet about your addiction to alcohol and the battle to recover could provide you with a new source of help, should you decide to share your story. It's not always a good idea to share your story with everyone you meet. But, the people you share with each other can be a potential source of encouragement. You might encounter someone else who is trying to quit drinking. It is possible to meet an alcoholic who has been cured of addiction. further along the road to recovery and could be a mentor for you.

Whichever path you decide to follow for your own recovery, you must choose a path that is right for you. Don't try to duplicate your experience of another. Perhaps you'll alter your own mental image that is in your head. This is a fantastic method to combat an image of yourself that is negative. It's not a crime for drinking more alcohol than you need to. You are actually having a personal issue which you would like to move beyond. Take care of yourself and avoid taking extreme measures unless you are forced to. One of the most important things to take note of the milestones in your life.

Recognize Milestones

The process of cutting down on alcohol isn't easy. There's withdrawal symptoms, family complaints as well as dangers for others and the harm done to your body. Once you've decided to end these habits, you're forced to change your habits and discover ways to cut out the alcohol from your life. It is crucial to acknowledge your achievements whenever they occur however small. This is the reason the reason Alcoholics Anonymous gives a 24-hour chip to its members. This small gesture is only the beginning of much.

The idea of recognizing or celebrating little milestones may appear odd to some, but it could be extremely beneficial. Retrospectively reviewing how far you've come can be more efficient when there's something important to be seen. Steps, landmarks or even events worthy of note may be different for each person. Certain, such as that first 24-hour period of recovery are definitely worth keeping track of. Other examples can be easily located by anyone who wants to search.

The first time that an addict asks an acquaintance or family member for assistance could merit acknowledgment. This is a sign of the addict's recognition that they're struggling and cannot overcome it completely by themselves. This is also a formal acknowledgment for the addiction support system. In reaching out to assistance the user is committing to utilize the assistance. Future actions will determine the frequency and how the addict will make use of their network.

Addicts often turn to their family or friends who are supportive to get their needs met. They might be able to lie to obtain the things they want, perhaps looking to get someone else to purchase alcohol on their behalf. This is not the right usage of a support system. This temptation can be too overwhelming for addicts who aren't. Because of this, it's worth looking into that the addict doesn't use their supportive friends to harm them or when they approach them with the right intention to help for the right reasons.

A better strategy to reach out to these friendly people could be such as calling them when you are really attracted. You could discuss what you feel and allow the conversation to shift into other areas in a natural way. It is important to change the direction of your thoughts. If you make a phone call to discuss your need to drink and then only talk about the subject for a prolonged period it might not help. The focus will remain of your problem, which means that you're thinking about it the same way as you did in the past. This means there is no changing of your thoughts or thoughts of the negative side effects of alcohol and no reminder of the motives that drove you to stop drinking initially. If you allow the conversation to flow freely, then talk about your problems to ensure they are dealt with, you could be able to return to more healthy habits.

Another important milestone to be cherished could include the very first occasion that that an individual who is an alcoholic does not purchase their favorite drink or, as it is often referred to, the first time to drive off. You can celebrate this decision to buy a drink, a sign that alcohol doesn't have any influence on them anymore. It is important to keep in mind that the various milestones and ways to celebrate them is personalized as required. When you are beginning your rehabilitation process, some individuals require a lot of milestones and progress to stay on track with the goal.

Other milestones include monitoring weight loss, which generally occurs early after the consumption of alcohol is reduced. It is common for people to lose a few pounds within their first week of fewer drinking. The timeline milestones also provide easy to identify: the first day, the first week, along with 30, 60 or 90 days. After the first week of having stopped drinking, alcohol-free drinkers must get their first restful night's sleep without any chemical interventions.

These milestones are able to be modified according to the needs. For instance, someone who drinks before dinner is looking to mark the first time they ate without alcohol. Someone who drinks in bars may be able to be celebrating when they first pass by it. They could decide to celebrate their first visit as the designated driver. It is possible to mark any milestone you wish however you want.

Milestones may also be celebrated by those who are cutting back on alcohol consumption instead of abstaining. It is possible to keep a count and attempt to spend on a specific number of days without drinking a set amount of drinks. If you are economically motivated, you may put aside the money they typically spent on alcohol and offer to donate the money. This approach is not recommended for those who's drinking has destroyed their finances. The money could go to a charity the addict dislikes with the money going into it if a portion of it goes to alcohol. This is radical way of changing the old ways of life and is not intended for anyone to try.

Each of these milestones is worthy of being recognized. It's not required to only occur once. Recovery is not without setbacks and there's no shame in that. People relapse, mistakes happen. It is possible to pick yourself up and begin again. Resetting your course does not derail your previous accomplishments. If you've been able to go a day without drinking for the first time and you're able to do it again. Even when you're facing setbacks, be sure to take time to celebrate the things you've achieved. It's possible!

## Chapter 9: Times To Determine When To Stop

### Drinking Alcohol

FROM USE TO ABUSE OF ALCOHOLIC BEVERAGES

More than 70% from the Spanish population drinks alcohol, but the majority of them don't suffer from alcohol-related issues or dependency. This legal depressant is usually associated with celebrations, social events and even free time. In this regard drinking alcohol may be misinterpreted as positive social behaviour, so long as it's taken in moderation.

The issue arises when someone drinks alcoholic drinks in a way that does not counteract anxiety. Also, for those with an alcohol dependence disorder also known as alcoholism, it is a way to drink is a way to lessen withdrawal symptoms. The specialist Enrique Echeburua reflects: People with drinking issues don't drink to feel better however, they drink to prevent feeling uncomfortable.

If we feel we have to consume alcohol in order to relax or cope with a negative situation, we're facing an issue. It is a reference to, in one way to drinking in excess within a short time. However drinking alcohol regularly in a regular manner, is considered to be a habit.

In both instances in both cases, if you consume it beyond set limits Ethyl liquor will begin to show signs of damage. It is a fact that all harmful substances affect the health and well-being of the person who consumes it, and is recognized in its biopsychosocial dimension. This is not just for the person however but also for individuals who surround him.

But, we aren't always aware of our flaws or excesses. This is why it's difficult to conclude that addiction or abuse of alcohol is happening. The affected person is usually the first to acknowledge it and relatives raise the alarm.

Below, we will examine the indicators that help answer the issue of how to identify if you're suffering from problems with alcohol.

A SMILE INSIGNS THAT DRINKING IS AVOID

Since it is a popular and popular drug like for alcohol It is not difficult to get into a pattern of abuse. It is generally accepted that drinking and drunkenness especially on weekends are considered to be normal. One could argue that our culture is a factor in this. Because it encourages us to drink as if it was an actual health issue.

Health professionals are aware that the first stage to develop alcoholism is the use of alcohol in a way that is harmful. This is thought to be a health risk and is more frequent than you believe. The popular notion of underestimating the amount of alcohol consumed and merely giving weight to the condition of alcoholism is a risky mistake.

This acceptance by society and concealing of the abuser's situation hinder early detection of the problem. The early detection of this problem will prevent more serious problems that are more than the alcohol-related disease. It will also prevent other kinds of social problems, such as traffic accidents, instances that involve violence, the emergence of related illnesses and loss of job, etc.

The warning signs to avoid the possibility of falling into a pattern drinking are:

* Drink regularly to attain the state of euphoria as well as diversion.

Drinking is an escape plan from challenging situations.

Consume large quantities of alcohol on your own.

* Drinking in unusual times and in unusual circumstances, e.g., in the morning, or in between meals.

Alcohol consumption without control and continuing drinking no matter how awful you feel in the post-hangover period.

Additionally the fact that we continue to drink even when it causes health issues or conflicts with others is a significant sign. This is a clear signification of the reality that we are losing control of our drinking habits and drink out of an obsession.

## SIGNS A COMMENT ALCOHOL DEPENDENCE IS DEVELOPED

In the above paragraph the frequency and amount of alcohol consumed could indicate the possibility of becoming addicted to alcohol. This is because drinking excessively within a short amount of time , and then continuing this habit in time may result in alcohol dependence.

One of the methods to determine if we are struggling with a drinking addiction problem is to show the following traits:

* Increase an aversion to alcohol. This means we have to consume more alcohol to get the desired effect.

* Feeling an urgent desire to drink, and drinking more often and over.

* Finding it difficult to quit drinking and taking in more alcohol than initially anticipated. This can include the idea to stop drinking but having no success in those efforts.

* Constantly time drinking alcohol and getting much longer recuperate from the consequences.

* Having withdrawal-related symptoms. This is psychological issues that cause anxiety, discomfort anger, depression, or handshakes

among others after the consumption has ended. Also, the need the urge to drink alcohol to relieve withdrawal symptoms.

* Experienced social, work or family events because of drinking. This could mean the end of important routines or activities and also instances of absence because of this dependency.

* Continue drinking alcohol regardless of the negative effects. This includes physical injuries and traffic accidents or accidents at work, disputes with others and inability to meet obligations, etc.

Noteable changes to personality. You may be more irritable, vulnerable and forgetful. You may also be weak with mood swings, etc.

If you've had at three or more of these issues within the last year, you've likely been a victim of the addiction spiral.

In Europe Alcohol is among of the most significant causes of premature deaths and morbidity. The negative effect it has on health and wellbeing is undisputed. It also affects not just those with an alcohol dependence disorders as well as those who do not consume alcohol regularly.

A few studies have revealed that the percentage of Spaniards who drink ethanol on an regular basis is among the highest levels in Europe. This is also the case for those who consume more than five alcohol-based drinks in the course of. In reality, it's believed that 10 percent of the population is suffering from addiction to alcohol.

When we speak about the dangers of alcohol-based substances or those with problems with drinking We think of alcoholism. We believe that only those who are addicted to the substance have health or behavior problems.

This is among the most common mistakes, and can make it difficult to establish the early signs of the drama. It is believed that people who drink alcohol in an excessive or abnormal manner, but with a sporadic pattern does not have an issue that is serious. However, this type of drinking is the cause of alcohol-related problems and can cause numerous personal and social dangers.

Alcohol-related risks manifest as illness, avoidable death as well as social issues, which can become an enigma for the public health. It is crucial to recognize the signs of reckless drinking as early as is possible and take action to address the problem.

But, treatment centers that are specialized can be found for those seeking assistance in kicking their habit of addiction and conquer the addiction problem. Abstinence and detoxification can help them. First, as an approach to manage withdrawal symptoms and relieve their symptoms. The second is as psychosocial processes that are based on psychotherapies, aid in preventing relapses. Through this assistance from professionals alcohol addicts are able to restore their life quality and their health.

## Chapter 10: Clear Alcohol Essation Goals Alcohol

## Cessation

THE VERY FIRST STEPS to take to quit ALCOHOL

It's not an easy task to stop drinking alcohol particularly if you're addicted to your drinking habits ... however, it's doable. It's just the first step towards achieving it.

Alcoholism is certainly one of the hardest addictions to stop. First, withdrawal symptoms can cause death in the event that it is not dealt with properly by experts , and gradually as well, and even after a person has come out of the addiction and becomes abstinent, it's likely to relapse as alcohol is an extremely accessible and affordable drug. For instance, the purchase of hard drugs such as cocaine or heroin can be expensive and difficult to come across but in Spain there is a bar in every corner, and at reasonable prices (in other countries, it's much more costly). It requires a lot of determination and a major alteration in your way of life.

If you've discovered that you are suffering from an addiction and are now determined to quit drinking completely ... congrats! You've already accomplished the most crucial thing: recognize the issue and take an informed decision. Here are some suggestions to help you.

The first step to stop drinking ALCOHOL

1. Do not attempt it on your own. If you've been dependent for a long period and you are unable to take it on by yourself, as it's extremely risky because of withdrawal-related symptoms. The best option is to be admitted to a therapy center for a short time or get outpatient treatment. There are also associations who are dedicated to this, and who can manage your case with a lower cost. If this doesn't make sense, you should at minimum, talk to your doctor so that they will be able to offer different options. Most likely, they will recommend you to psychiatry and prescribe psychotropic medication that will aid in reducing withdrawal symptoms. Most commonly, benzodiazepines are prescribed that reduce anxiety symptoms.

2. Be conscious and commit to yourself. It is important to take a look at your experience and appreciate every benefit you receive when you quit drinking, including an improved quality of life physically and mentally. Make an inventory of all negative elements that you'll put down once you have stopped drinking. You can keep it in a prominent spot in your house. It is also beneficial to read at least once on the adverse effects that alcohol has on your body You'll be amazed to learn the number of ailments directly connected to alcoholism.

However inform all significant people you have in your lives of the choice you made , so that they are able to assist you. This will boost your commitment. You must also take things little by little to stopping drinking, starting by decreasing your consumption until the point is reached when you must end your drinking completely. Set realistic goals.

3. Accept that you are suffering from some issues. A lot of people think that alcoholism is a simple black and white issue. You either are an alcoholic, portrayed as the standard image of one who

drinks every day or not. But the reality is more complicated and many who drink drinks on a regular basis but not to the extent that they do and if they are causing a issue in their life, need professional assistance.

While the expression "the initial step to take is to admit you're suffering" may sound like a cliché but the reality is that it can be extremely helpful in the recovery process of an alcoholic.

If you notice that you're obsessing over the amount of alcohol you consume and if you find yourself comparing yourself with a friend over it, or think that drinking alcohol makes it difficult to live the life you'd like to lead You must take action since it's a clear issue for you, and definitely for your family members.

4. Do a general cleanse. Eliminate all forms of alcohol out of your house and don't find reasons to keep even a single bottle or can. Some people make the argument that if they've got guests visiting, they must be able to provide them with at least one drink. Forget it! When your visitors are significant enough for you to be, they'll know that you won't be serving alcohol in your home.

Provide them with other drinks like juices or soft drinks.

5. Inform your friends about your plans. Inform your friends that you've decided to cut down on alcohol consumption. Tell them that you are trying to be healthier will assist you in being more conscientious and more dedicated to your goals.

It can also inspire your friends and family to be willing to assist you and help them understand the seriousness of the situation. This way you can request your friends and family not to serve alcohol or wine during celebrations, or suggest that you organize activities in which there is alcohol-free.

6. Write down your reasons for doing this. Stopping drinking offers both the short and long-term advantages However, most people prefer immediate results instead of months of waiting to see results.

It's hard to progress when you're not sure what you're doing or the reason behind it. Note down on a piece paper the reasons you're trying to quit or reduce your intake of alcohol and place them in a prominent spot in your kitchen or bedroom.

A few of the advantages of quitting drinking alcohol for a short time include the ability to have conversations that are more clear and engaging without drinking excessively or wasting time with hangovers, or getting better sleep.

7. There is no alcohol in the home. This may sound like a simple and however an extreme step but the reality is that it's the most effective way to stay clear of drinking alcohol at home. Eliminate all alcohol and should you need to, if needed remove scents and drugs that contain the substance.

You'll be a bit embarrassed about your money, but remember that you're doing it to protect your health. All that money you've thrown away could benefit you over time by not going to the doctor to treat liver issues or paying penalties for driving while under drunk.

Soft drinks aren't the best choice. A person who is an alcoholic and whose preferred drink is beer changing to non-alcoholic beverages is not going to help you stop drinking, but on the contrary, you'll think you're drinking something that doesn't have the flavor to give beer the distinctive taste and you'll want to drink more.

8. You should consider joining an Alcoholics Anonymous type group. It's a great aid because you'll meet others who are in a similar position similar to yours. This will allow you to understand the situation and you'll also be given an "sponsor" that you can count on should you'd like to vent or need assistance. Through a support group, the rate of success is more than 80 percent, compared to 25% of people who attempt to quit by themselves.

9. Drinking diary. This method can be very useful in putting the amount of alcohol you consume into the proper perspective. It is recommended to write it down the initial three or four weeks after you've decided to quit drinking all the alcohol you consume.

In a journal each day, record how many glasses you had and what kind of alcohol you consumed as well as the location and time you had it in addition to noting the way you felt and with whom you shared your drinks with.

This will let you examine in greater detail which situations you drink in when you've cut off in the past month, and also who the people are who encourage drinking.

10. Social relationships are changing. Many drinkers will be forced to close the section of their life, and even leave the friends they have had a relationship with for a time. While you may not meet them again, but be aware that at a minimum for a period of time, it is suggested to stay clear of these people. If you have a habit of drinking with some people, the urge are likely to come back when you come across them because you've long associated the person with drinking. Similar to ex-smokers, former smokers experience a similar feeling when they see acquaintances who used to smoke They feel more compelled to smoke.

Tell them about the issue and if they truly love them, they'll understand and help you from a distance. Once you've had a while, and you feel better then you can begin to rekindle the relationship. But do not attempt to "make" those who are abstinence because trying to persuade people to stop drinking when they aren't aware that they have a problem is like telling someone who has fear of heights to take an elevator that is small. The best method to assist them is to demonstrate in time how you're doing and how you've managed your time since then they will begin to notice.

11. Determine what brought you to this point. The motives that brought you to rely on alcohol may be numerous and diverse. Identifying each one requires some deep reflection.

It can be helpful to create a an inventory of all the circumstances, locations, people and the reasons that led to your drinking.

It is essential to keep track of the way you felt prior to as well as after you had a drink in all of the situations. A night out with your friends for celebrating isn't the same as drinking at home on your own after a fight with your spouse.

This allows the psychologist to develop strategies for dealing with stressful situations and to avoid drinking alcohol.

12. You should take time off. Start seeking out activities or interests that will fill your time were

drinking. Many former drinkers admit that they relapsed because their house was destroyed by the fall. When you suffer from alcoholism, you often are unable to work and spend the majority of the time in their homes, which can be extremely boring and overwhelming The temptations to drink are on an all-time level. Reconnect with the things you used take pleasure in or find new activities that satisfy your needs.

13. Avoid substituting substitutes for alcohol. Do not engage in any activity, eat or other drinks. In this case, I am referring to that you are not drinking or eating or engaging in an exercise in excess until you become obsessed with it. There are those who, because of quitting drinking alcohol, drink binge drinks or drink different types of unhealthy drinks. Other people however become addicted to different kinds of behavior that can be problematic when they are consumed time spent online, such as, for instance, spending hours online (chat rooms or gambling and online video games and more. ).

14. Learn to say no. Drinking alcohol is a common practice in our culture, therefore it's difficult to

resist the temptation of a drinker. There could be a scenario that someone asks for and demands drinks.

In this kind of scenario, it's crucial to take the person serving us drinks straight in the face and then with a serious yet friendly and courteous manner make a quick and clear "no thanks".

Don't give inordinate explanations or a lengthy answer. If you have a trusted acquaintance who knows about the issue, request that they assist you in dealing with the issue together.

15. Don't give up. It will be difficult to stop drinking and you'll probably fall back during the course of your journey. But, you shouldn't abandon the fight, you must persevere each day. If, for whatever reason, you make a mistake, don't blame yourself or rant about it constantly We are all human, and we make mistakes. However it is possible to try to avoid the pitfalls. For instance, if you already know that you could encounter a dangerous situation, you should write on a small piece of paper a brief self-learning checklist (which you must keep in a place that is easily accessible and that you are able to

read quickly) of the things you'll should do to help you overcome the situation safely and avoid the consumption.

16. Give yourself a reward. It is crucial to realize how difficult it is to break an addiction. For this reason, if you do make gains, it's important rewarding yourself with a certain manner.

Naturally, these benefits cannot include alcohol However, you will be able to purchase a variety of items using the money you've been able to save through not having to spend each month on alcohol.

17. Rehabilitation. Sometimes even if you see a specialist stopping smoking is impossible.

It could be due to the fact that our environment doesn't allow it, our family members also have issues with alcohol or because we lack the determination, health may decline and leave us with the impression that there is no way to fix it.

It is for this reason that there are places in which it is possible to be completely away from the world, without the temptation on fingertips, and with supervision of addiction specialists.

Remember that it's not too late stop drinking alcohol, even in the most severe cases of cirrhosis. Quitting alcohol will result in more than significant improvement in the individual.

## Chapter 11: Consult A Dentist

What is the best time to see a DOCUMENTARY?

Many addicts to alcohol do not acknowledge that they are unable to manage their drinking. If alcohol consumption becomes an issue, it is recommended to seek medical assistance.

MINIMIZING and DENYING - IF there is no perspective

The main issue with alcoholism is denial on part of the affected which is a significant factor. "I don't have any issues in drinking!" Many alcoholics would declare. So, those with issues with alcohol rarely visit doctors independently.

Family members frequently deny or deny the problem of alcohol. They're allowing addiction to alcohol through ignoring the issue or by taking responsibility for their family's financial and personal situation. Sometimes, what's known as codependency can occur. In many instances the use of alcohol can be kept from caregivers and family members for a lengthy period of duration of.

## SIGNS EARLY AND SYMPTOMS

When confronted with their drinking issue, addicts to alcohol typically deny the existence of their problem. It is an complicated illness that is typically characterized by the character of the individual affected as well as other external factors. Thus, signs and symptoms vary between individuals. However, certain behavior patterns and indicators could indicate the presence of a drinking issue.

Examples include irritability, anxiety or insomnia, frequent falls , other injuries, many bruises as well as chronic depression, absence from school or work or work, loss of job divorce or separation, difficulties with finances frequently increases in weight, and auto accidents.

## SYMPTOMS AND LATE SIGNS

Signs and symptoms that are late may include the following conditions:

* Pancreas inflammation (pancreatitis)

* Non-organic digestive disorders (functional dyspepsia)

* Liver disease attributed to alcohol

* Nerve damage (polyneuropathy)

* Anemia (anemia)

* Brain damage

* Brain function abnormalities (in extreme cases, Wernicke Korsakoff syndrome)

* Stomach ulcers

* There is bleeding in the stomach.

Children of parents who drink are more likely to getting addicted to substances like alcohol or drugs, and subsequently developing anxiety, behavior disorders and emotional issues.

Alcohol dependence is closely connected to suicide-related psychological disorders and comorbidities. People often feel ashamed embarrassed, ashamed, and depressed, especially if the addiction to alcohol has led to major losses like B. Friendships, work social standing as well as physical and mental health. A variety of medical issues are caused by or worsened due to drinking alcohol. Furthermore, many dependent sufferers are not able to adhere with the prescribed medication.

It's usually an employee or family member who convinces or pressures the individual in question to seek medical assistance. Even if a person with a problem is able to begin therapy without pressure from relatives, employers or physicians, this could still result in successful outcomes. Therapy can inspire those affected to address their drinking problem.

## MEDICINE PROBLEMS

The consumption of alcohol can cause many alcohol-related ailments which require urgent medical attention.

### Injuries

Alcohol is a major cause of a number of falls, traffic accidents and other incidents (e.g. drowning) as well as fires and thefts. In these situations it is imperative to seek immediate assistance. The majority of the time drunks are in a condition where they are unable to judge the severity of the injury. For instance injuries that can result in serious injury could be ignored.

## ALCOHOL WITHDRAWAL

If an individual who is dependent on alcohol stops drinking, withdrawal symptoms that are severe can occur. They need to be assessed by a doctor and then treated. In general withdrawal symptoms are manifested by tremors, restlessness in the body and sweating. There are also confusion, sleep disturbances hallucinations, epileptic seizures.

"* Tremors: At this point it is evident that the hands and legs move frequently. It is evident by asking the person to extend their hands or to hold them. When they tremor, there is intense anxiety and restlessness and usually sweating, sleep disturbances nausea, vomiting, and even loss of appetite can occur.

"Epileptic seizures" ("convulsions") are a symptom that occurs in the event that withdrawal signs are extreme. When an epileptic seizures occurs, the patient is unconscious and suffers generalized cramps throughout the body. It's hard to know how many patients with alcohol dependence suffered from epileptic seizures in withdrawal, however these seizures are common among high-risk individuals.

If you observe an epileptic seizure you must lay the patient on their backs following the seizure to ensure that vomit does not enter the lungs and cause breathing difficulties. If you can, take care to shield the person's head and body parts from damage due to the flooring or objects. It is possible to do this by moving furniture or objects blocking the path. You can try something gentle such as B. to slip an object under your head. However, it is not recommended to be able to hold the person experiencing convulsions or hold head as it could increase the risk of injuries. Don't put any object in the mouth of the person who is having an epileptic seizures!

* Hallucinations can occur for those who are extremely dependent on alcohol, and are usually part of the symptoms of Delirium Tremens (severe withdrawal from alcohol). Most people have reported that worms or insects creep on walls or on the skin. It is possible to "feel" animals ' skin. Certain patients have reported "hearing" certain things however it isn't as prevalent. Optic

hallucinations are more frequent when you are suffering from withdrawal.

* Delirium tremens is one of the more severe kind of withdrawal-related symptoms. The condition is much less frequent than epileptic seizures. It is only seen in those who drink heavily. The condition typically occurs between within 48-72 hours of the last drink. A severe confusion (delirium) occurs when one is suffering from withdrawal. The person is awake, but extremely confused. In the same moment the person experiences the sensation of delirium, motorization sweating, hallucinationsand palpitations, and elevated blood pressure. This is a life-threatening condition. If untreated the chance of dying is extremely high, however when medical treatment is administered properly in the hospital, the chance of death is extremely low in the present.

ALCOHOLIC KETOACIDOSIS

Alcoholic ketoacidosis (AKD) is a serious rare and rare condition that has to be treated promptly. It usually manifests within two to four days of the last time you drank alcohol. A majority of patients suffer from acute pancreatitis due to the result of acute pancreatitis. They also suffer intense abdominal pain that was triggered by small amounts of fluid and food for several days. Acute withdrawal symptoms and ketoacidosis could occur at the at the same time. The condition can cause nausea vomiting, abdominal pain dehydration, as well as an acetone-like smell within the atmosphere. The reason is due to the loss of the individual's water and carbohydrate reserves. In this way, the body's body burns off proteins and fats, which produces keto bodies. They are acidic substances that accumulate in blood, and they lower the pH of blood. Acidosis (overacidification of blood) occurs. It can cause discomfort. The people affected drink and eat less which, in turn, increases symptoms of the illness.

AUTOTHER MENTAL illness

Alcohol dependence is frequently linked to mental health issues like depression, anxiety as well as psychosis (delusions or hallucinations). These mental disorders, which are often coupled with impaired judgment when the alcohol-induced state, can raise the likelihood to commit suicide or attempt suicide or other suicide-related behaviors among people who drink. If someone has committed suicide in the past or may be at risk of trying suicide seeking medical attention, assistance should be sought out as soon as it is possible.

The ailments mentioned here pertain to ailments that should be addressed by an emergency doctor. Additionally, a variety of ailments can worsen with continuous consumption of alcohol, for example, liver cirrhosis and hepatocellular carcinoma. Other cancers, nervous system diseases, and more.

Do you have a DRINKING Problem?

There are a variety of questions you could ask yourself or someone you suspect to be an alcohol user to determine the extent of their consumption. This test , known as CAGE can be used for self-assessment and is not a diagnostic aid.

Ask these questions:

Have ever thought about having a healthier lifestyle?

Have you ever felt irritated by criticisms from your peers regarding your drinking habits?

Did you have any guilt for drinking?

Have you ever had a glass of before you went to work in order to help you get started and ease your stress?

If all four questions are answered by"yes," then "yes," alcohol addiction is presumed.

GET HELP!

The addiction to alcohol is a narcotic disorder. As with all diseases there are treatment options for this condition that must be employed. The secondary illness as well as the social aspect and the breakdown of family structures because of drinking, all of it should be ignored. Your doctor can help.

CONSULTING WITH SENTIIVE QUESTIONS: ALCOHOL CONSUMPTION

When it comes to sensitive subjects, you must cross the threshold of inhibition regardless of whether you're discussing death, sexuality or addiction. There is something personal and personal about these matters which is why the person who is concerned needs "permission" to discuss the subject. If the patient is scared and is scared, they will try to shield himself or herself and close down. Thus the family doctor who is trusted is trained to maneuver through the problem area and respect the uniqueness of each patient.

WHAT MUCH is TOO MUCH

Based on current data from epidemiology that most adults don't consume alcohol or engage in moderate risk drinking. Dangerous, dangerous, and dependent drinkers have a medical or psychiatric importance. Alcohol consumption. Risky drinking is defined as continuous (near) drinking alcohol on a daily basis that can increase the danger of physical injury, e.g., liver cirrhosis. However, as of the date that it was diagnosed, has not yet experienced negative psychological, physical, or social implications. Experts differ on what level that alcohol consumption is to be harmful to health. Certain experts define dangerous drinking as drinking more than four standard drinks a each day for males and more than two drinks for women. In some instances drinking daily quantities of more than two drinks of standard for males as well as more than one drink that is considered standard for women is considered to be risky. The term "binge-drinking" refers to having four normal drinks and more on a single night for women and or five normal drinks, or even more so for guys. A normal drink, for instance is 0.3 1 l of alcohol or 0.1 L of wine, and is composed of between 10-12 grams of alcohol in pure form.

If alcohol abuse has already caused the physical or mental health. However, the conditions for addiction syndrome aren't satisfied. In the case of dependent as per ICD-10 (F.10.2) the alcohol consumption is characterized by symptoms of psychological dependence, such as an intense desire for alcohol or the loss of control over the duration of consumption, or even the final twelve months prior to diagnosis. consumed or signs of physical dependence like the signs of withdrawal when drinking ceases and the increase in tolerance i.e. the necessity from the standpoint of the person in question to increase the dosage of alcohol to obtain the desired psychotropic effects.

The withdrawal symptoms and the development of tolerance result of the brain's adaptation to drinking. Questions like the AUDIT aid in defining the problem with alcohol.

EPIDEMIOLOGY, CONSEQUENCES and the importance of excessive alcohol CONSUMPTION

The statistics show that in Germany, 1.8 million people depend on alcohol. It is a mental illness that is associated with a high degree of genetic predisposition, which can lead to problems with health, workplace and family problems. There are serious effects of drinking excessively for the entire society (traffic accidents, crimes and lost work). Alcohol consumption that is excessive causes indirect and direct costs of around 26.7 billion euros to Germany's economy. German economy. Over 90 percent of addicts do not receive treatment for addiction currently. Prevention and reduction of harm from alcohol are among the top problems facing society today.

TREATMENT

For alcohol-dependent patients, treatment specialized for them is recommended that includes therapeutic elements like withdrawal treatment and abstinence therapy. When it comes to withdrawal treatment (mostly for patients admitted to hospitals) the withdrawal disorder is alleviated by taking medications. Any physical or mental disease is identified and treatment begins. The patient is enticed to seek treatment after withdrawal to help build an abstinence life. This could mean an inpatient treatment to stop abstinence at an addiction clinic with specialized expertise for a period of time. Meanwhile, there are also outpatient psychiatric offers for abstinence-oriented treatment, sometimes with the use of abstinence-supportive medications such as acamprosate, naltrexone, and nalmefene.

The family doctor, particularly, plays an important role to play in identifying the issue of alcohol and suggesting treatment. There's a broad and diverse network of counseling facilities for addiction, certified withdrawal treatment centers as well as addiction clinics. A number of places have also added outpatient therapy services in recent times. If a physician is successful engaging in short interventions to get the addict to visit an addiction counseling facility or specific treatment for addiction, a lot has been achieved. The family doctor should be aware and inform the patient that the effectiveness of treatment for alcohol-related patients at a clinic that is specialized is far superior to what is usually believed. This is particularly applicable to patients who have employment and a well-established social network. The follow-up exams that follow up show high the success rate. The role of the GP is to encourage and support you to pursue this long-term path that is promising.

In accordance with the current AWMF guidelines for the management of disorders involving alcohol the effectiveness of short interventions for the vast majority of individuals who aren't (yet) dependent however, are at-risk drinkers has been demonstrated with strong evidence and they are suggested to be provided by general physicians. One of the primary benefits of a physician-led intervention would be that the issue with alcohol is acknowledged (with the aid by screening tools, among others) as well as the client is educated. Family members could also give an opportunity for discussion about the use of alcohol. This is why it can be helpful to engage the entire family members or a close friend. However, this is offset with the reality that family members tend to cover up the fact that a family member is dependent because of shame, and they do all they can.

ACTION

The family physician is not the first doctor to be consulted for alcohol-related problems or physical ailments, but rather for physical issues that may, nevertheless could be the result of an excessive consumption of alcohol. As part of the explanation of these complaints, issues with alcohol consumption may be discussed. If, from the doctor's perspective it is evident that there's an alcohol issue the doctor should set aside adequate time for this discussion. The patient should be provided with an opportunity to discuss his situation and the doctor should be given the chance to ask questions and provide additional suggestions. The process of diagnosing and classifying the severity of alcohol-related problems is a process that focuses on two things

On one hand exploring the current situation and, on the other hand, a record of the desire to transform an alcohol-related problem into a serious issue.

The doctor may start the conversation as follows: "You gave me important details about your health habits like alcohol consumption, physical activity as well as smoking practices. This shouldn't be taken as a given, so thank you! I'd like to speak with you about this briefly Do I believe that you are right?"

Short interventions based on fundamentals of Motivational Interviewing. They are ideal for consultations with physicians in clinical practice. These small interventions aid the physician determine how much they are able to motivate the patient to alter his behaviour and the best way to assist him in this. Contrary to paternalistic medical communication, which may be perceived as a patronizing approach in the sense that it dictates what should be done for the patient "motivational interviews" (MI) concentrates on empowering the patient's capabilities. The principles of discussion in MI are based on the belief that the patient can make behavior change that is suitable for them (self-efficacy) and is accountable for the change. The physician is able to start change processes without wishing to expose or punish the patient. make the results of medical research, e.g. laboratory results related to the consumption of alcohol (feedback) and encourage the patient to consider the implications of these results for his consumption of alcohol. The doctor is well-versed in local assistance and is able to explain their distinctive particularities. The discussion is based on a sensitivity empathy (empathy) of the patient's situation and challenges in changing their behavior. However, ultimately the patient decides the amount and type of behavioral changes he wants to tackle. The doctor will determine the stage of change his the patient is at and determines the objectives of the meeting and avoids unnecessary interventions, such as regarding the actual starting of abstinence-oriented therapy in cases where the patient is not able to receive this.

If a patient is clear that he/she would rather not enter into the consultation process (for at least a while) the doctor should take this into consideration. However this approach is not unimportant, since the patient may feel that his doctor is willing to discuss the issue of drinking with him. Another crucial principle is to not view the relapses as failures, neither for the physician, nor on behalf of the individual. Relapses are a an element of change and may be utilized for a new start by implementing the appropriate adaption.

Because motivational discussions can take longer, it's beneficial to contact the patient at a short time. Avoid unnecessary consultations where the doctor asks questions that are dismissive or provides a sloppy advice. The goal is usually to emphasize that both the patient and physician have recognized the issue and that the issue has been clearly and unambiguously mentioned in name and that the doctor is committed to the willingness to take action.

## Conclusion

"Unless your sober existence is more important than your drinking life then you'll relapse. You decide what life is important to you. ."--Toni Sorenson

Alcohol is among the most accepted addictive substances that exist similar to nicotine and caffeine. A lot of people fall under the trap, and each one has their own motives to do so. This could be for any reason. Perhaps your finances are struggling or your family's life isn't as peaceful. Maybe you're just looking to improve your health. The reason you quit drinking is more or less important than the other.

If you decide to quit or cut back or cutting back, you'll face obstacles which you'll need to get over. They could be self-defeating or buying alcohol you don't really need or as a result of family members or friends who don't understand. This is a frequent problem because alcoholism is well-known and accepted. People who don't experience problems in the first place tend to ignore these issues or don't think about them. Why is that? If the problem you're facing isn't a direct danger or cause disruption to the person concerned, then why should they be concerned? Spending too much cash on a beer will not affect the ability of your neighbor to pay their expenses.

If you're a relative or friend of an addict trying to get better You must be cautious about how you talk about things about them. Do not inquire about when they'll be recovering for. Don't be angry in the event that they're not making the improvement you think they should be. If you've signed up for call at night, make certain not to grumble or make comments such as "here we come again" when you respond to the phone. These kinds of actions could trigger negative thoughts, and even a return to addiction in your addiction. If you're the only person they seek therapy from, be there for them and assist in distracting them. The person with addiction issues in your life may be enthused by the opportunity to distract them. Follow their example.

The reduction in drinking offers many advantages that are associated with it, such as greater mental and physical health. No one starts drinking since things are being good within their life. These are more of than a plea for assistance. If family and friends know the signs to look for, they might be able to prompt early intervention. It's more of a wishful-thinking approach more than anything, but. In general, people who are alcoholics aren't noticed until something major takes place. A bar fight, or accident could be the trigger that draws the attention of family members.

In the midst of alcohol's widespread acceptance within the society and the general tendency to worry over themselves and their own lives, presence of your family or friends with your drinking habits is an indication that something has to change. It could be that you are paying for things your family doesn't have. You may be fooling yourself. In certain extreme situations your family might be afraid of them. In any case, stay assured that things will improve regardless of what the situation are right at present.

But, making a change to the right direction could not be able to sustain your routines. There are alcoholics who have to undergo a complete overhaul of their lives to fully recover. It is a complicated procedure. But, regardless of regardless of whether you've got a foundation set up or you are beginning with a new foundation, addicts are faced with the same challenges.

Abstaining from alcohol or even reducing how much you drink, could be a difficult task. It is essential to stay in control as much as you can. If you opt to include aside alcohol-free days in your calendar make sure you don't make them excuses to indulge in a frenzied lifestyle for the remainder throughout the entire week. Also, you must be open with yourself about your drinking routines. This will allow you to determine what you need to change and what is able to remain the same.

Changes in habits aren't easy for everyone, but there are strategies available to assist addicts. If you're not willing to pass by a place that you frequent, modify your route. If you're still in need of get together with colleagues then you could suggest a new location. If it's the bar, ask to serve as the designated driver. Every issue has a solution If you're willing to find it.

## Resources All Around

Many resources are available to those who wish to decrease or stop an addiction to alcohol. There are numerous therapies available to assist in overcoming withdrawal symptoms, the temptations, and rethinking the way you think about alcohol. A lot of therapists accept health insurance. In the worst case scenario one could be placed in a center by the recommendation of other people. But, this is only in situations where the person is at a high danger to themselves and those who are around them. The majority of those who are seeking to treat and get better aren't placed in a situation where they are being held against their own will.

The process of overcoming your addiction, and recognizing indicators and triggers that can set your off are fantastic assignments to work on with the help of a professional trained. They can help you recognize the risk factors, habits and triggers that could be able to change the way you think about it. When you are working on an action plan in conjunction with your counsellor, it's essential to be transparent and open about your life and emotions emotionally and physically. Being honest is essential in any rehabilitation.

It is also essential to identify the type of therapy you're at ease with. Many prefer having one-on-one sessions, where they do not be concerned about any judgements regarding their speech. The concept of behavioral therapy is also appealing to many as it allows you to change the way you live your life in a logic-based causal method. If I stop at an gas station, then I'll purchase soda instead of a beer. This kind of habit can make the task of cutting back more simple.

Certain people perform better when they are in a group. They rely on their group for a sense that they are accountable. You could claim that you're not in therapy to help yourself. You'll be able to observe what Sam is doing and what Anne may be wearing. Any excuse or reason that can convince you to go with a positive outlook is fine. Like the decision to reduce your alcohol intake the intention and effort will be the most important factors.

Sometimes, the intention could be completely selfish, provided that it's working for you. Perhaps you continue to attend Alcoholics Anonymous meetings just to evaluate your sober days to someone who was there the week before you. It is not a good idea to turn this into any sort of long-term contest, particularly since you're only competing with yourself, but if this kind thought makes you work hard and change your behavior in the beginning you should be good. The only person that needs to be aware of this type of motivation, and when it does work, it is effective.

Even if you don't choose to attend therapy, it does not mean that you are on your own in your endeavors. Family members and friends willing to listen may be able to help. Twelve-step programs can give you the feeling of being accountable to other people who share the same values. You could even create security measures against yourself by limiting the amount you can spend or the amount of alcohol you're allowed to purchase. If you choose to do this, you can decide to share these established limits with a trusted friend to add an additional level of accountability.

It is essential to maintain that honesty in oneself and also honesty with other people. For those who are interested the standard drinking amount is twelve ounces alcohol, 5 ounces wine or one and a half ounces of liquor that is hard to find. Monitoring how much you're actually drinking has been proven to be an eye-opener for some. It can also provide you with a an efficient and simple method to recognize your successes in the event that the amount you drink daily decreases.

Whichever method of treatment you decide to pursue You can keep track of the progress you've made in that process. This can assist those who are struggling to see progress in their efforts. There are six stages to recovering from alcohol. Each stage looks on the relation between the alcohol user and the addict. The initial stages are filled with excuses as the addict hasn't accepted the severity of their addiction yet.

Stage one is referred to as precontemplation. At this point the person who is addicted isn't likely to seek treatment without any external influence. They don't suffer from a problem, are fully in control of their alcohol intake, and are completely in the game of defending themselves. They're likely to be suffering from the negative effects of their degree of alcohol intake they're at, yet they are unwilling to acknowledge that they have problems. Alcohol addicts who are in the recovery phase tend to be reluctant to talk about their addiction and attempt to divert conversation. Understanding and patience is the only ways to get beyond this stage.

Family and family members is vital in this phase because the person who is alcoholic is likely to make excuses. The people they have close to them could be a source of motivation to seek assistance. This is a tricky balance to achieve however if they are able to keep the thought of seeking help in all times in an alcohol-dependent mind, this could occur eventually. So long as they don't try to hinder the person from moving away from the thought that they are suffering from problems, further involvement will only cause the next stage earlier.

The next step is to consider. In this stage, people may realize they are suffering however they may not realize the severity of it. Stalling is commonplace in this stage. The addict is likely to eventually seek help, but it will be a couple of months. There is no commitment to taking any concrete actions. Many people remain in this state of recovery for a long period of time and not want to make any progress, and make excuses for their drinking habits and deny the seriousness of their issue.

The process of contemplation can be a challenging step for people who are who are close to an alcoholic. Being aware of the issue and seeing how serious it is aren't the same. Reminders could be helpful, but they also can cause harm. There's always a way when dealing with alcohol users. Being too aggressive may seem like an attack, however any weak strategy can be dismissed as being insignificant. Communication is crucial and that's the reason why tools like group therapy as well as family therapy are able to be helpful tremendously.

The third stage is known as preparation. In this stage the addict is committed to change their lifestyle to better. Planning is essential at this point. The addict must spend time looking at their habits, and develop specific alternatives to prevent from reverting to previous habits. People who fail to attend this critical plan stage tend to fall short with an actionable plan in place. The process can take between 18 and 18 months. It involves all the changes in behavior and staying clear of triggers that have been previously discussed.

This is a time where the addition of another could cause more harm than positive. The addict is aware of their circumstances the best, their addiction, and their thoughts the most effective. They have to figure out their own plans for how they are feasible in order to reduce their dependence and what they should do when temptation strikes the most hard. The idea of having someone highlight the difficulties they face in battling an addiction they're not having or trying to cut down will only add more workload and burdens for the person who is alcoholic. There isn't a need to undertake complete reform in all aspects of an alcoholic's life. Simple steps are essential and crucial.

Maintenance represents the sixth step. It is the point where all plans and the new habits gradually become routine. Implementing healthy strategies for coping and pursuing new interests are essential to getting through this phase. Once the addict has overcome the addiction issue, they will be able to reap the benefits of sobriety. It is also the time the time when organ damage starts to heal itself, if that the addict has abstained for long enough.

In this phase when the involvement of other people is likely to be an immense aid. If the addict is able to get an understanding of their new behavior it is not necessary to fret about massive Relapses. Families and friends need to keep in mind that relapses can happen at any point and must be able to accept them with encouragement to press the reset button to begin again. The simple act of pointing out the advantages of sobriety, or more subtle gestures such as spending more time with an addict and as they less drink will help reinforce the reason to cut back on drinking. These reminders are positive when an addict examines their past to be able to see how far they've progressed in their recovery.

The last stage is referred to as the termination stage and there are a myriad of theories about the concept of termination. Many people believe that addiction to alcohol is a lifetime issue and cite evidence that addicts display certain behavior even when alcohol is not within their system. Dry drinking and can be seen in behaviors like insanity and dysfunction. Many claim that the existence of these traits proves alcohol addiction does not ever truly disappear. However, in reality at this point the addict is no longer having a desire to drink and thus is totally cured.

Behaviors that are impulsive and problematic are the most important thing to look out for. Anyone with an addictive personality or genetic predisposition to alcohol use may go from cutting back on alcohol to engaging in other addiction. Smoking, gambling or taking illegal drugs are only a few possible options. Instinctive behavior for recovering alcohol addicts could include excessive spending or making snap-decisions that are unhealthy, or things like embracing an addiction.

Even something healthy, such as exercise, could be harmful when it's not done in moderate amounts. Inability to moderate determines the format and structure of the life of an addict however, it doesn't necessarily have to last forever.

For a Brighter Future

Reducing your alcohol consumption could be difficult however, everyone has a motive to keep striving. The prospect of earning more income, healthier and a peaceful life at home could be the reason that keeps your spirits up. A less alcoholic lifestyle can boost your chances of advancing in your career as well. It's as easy as having no hangovers in the morning, or a time of sleep that is peaceful can suffice to attract attention. Whatever motivates you to work hard is sufficient.

Let people know about the work you're doing. Let your family and friends know about it. Establish your support network early to ensure that any person who might be troublesome is able to come out. If you know someone who has said they'll be supportive of your efforts to reduce alcohol consumption however, they then offer the opportunity to buy each round or show up at your home with a 12 pack This isn't anyone you should have in your network of support. Be sure to mention how your actions have a negative impact on you, and ask them whether they're willing to modify or end contact however long you're competent. It may seem like a harsh decision however, adding more opportunities for temptations will just make it more difficult for you.

Be sure to communicate your concerns clearly with the people around you. If you have specific nights when you're not drinking to avoid alcohol, invite your family friends or frequent visitors to the household to be a part of your celebration. Making a list of activities will help you stay off temptation. A evening of family games or a stroll around the neighborhood could help you forget about your troubles. It is also possible that your family is content to be spending time with you who is sober.

Remember that your family members are trying to figure this out with you and everyone is trying to find out how living that is alcohol-free can work. They might want to speak with you about their experiences about your drinking. Do this only in the presence of a qualified counselor or when you are confident enough to handle the consequences, particularly in the beginning. If you have a friend or family member who is looking to talk, offer them the opportunity to talk and don't consider yourself to take on their burdens in your own. If the conversation gets disturbing or disturbs you excessively, you have every right to leave. Perhaps suggest someone else they can talk to, for instance, an acquaintance who sympathizes with their issues.

If you're a recovering alcoholic it is important to put your personal care first. If you're in need of the dry days, make use of these days and don't be embarrassed about it. If you must attend therapy at least twice a month, go ahead and be honest and open about what you're experiencing. If you are required to spend time in a parking lot for a few minutes contemplating whether or not to go inside and purchase alcohol, go ahead and be proud as you leave empty handed. Be sure that your needs are being met.

Being healthier in your mind will lead to bigger and better things over time. Actually, the enhancements of your physical and mental health are closely linked. Being healthier means you have more energy, which is a result of increased levels of endorphins in your brain and improved mood all around. This is all the result of slow progress. The initial two beers less a week could lead to the reduction of six drinks. Participating in support groups can provide you more interaction with other people who have similar struggles. In the future, you could even be in a position of mentorship in helping others who are in search of recovery.

This goal might not be suitable for everyone, but often these goals can be achieved. You could set out to cut down on one six-pack every week of what you drink on a regular basis. If you limit the amount of your normal drinks by drinking a glass, or a can at each at a time, your body begins to notice the changes. Less headaches, less hangovers and less harm for your brain only the beginning of the place you could be. When you have eliminated the first six-pack you've ever had and you may come across another person who is struggling with their own battle. If you're able to offer assistance with your advice and knowledge, you might be a motivational source. You could keep cutting down on alcohol in order to demonstrate to others that you can achieve the same results.

Be aware that each person has their own motives and what motivates you could not be the same for another person's circumstances. Don't let someone else's failure affect yours and do not let yourself slip off the track due to someone else's success. Keep your objectives in your mind and resist letting tempting thoughts pull you away frequently. Accept setbacks and be willing to rise and go for it again.

www.ingramcontent.com/pod-product-compliance
Lightning Source LLC
Chambersburg PA
CBHW050400120526
44590CB00015B/1760